NEWTON FREE LIBRARY
W9-AYE-923

# Native Americans of California

## Titles in the Indigenous Peoples of North America Series Include:

The Apache
The Blackfeet
The Cherokee
The Cheyenne
The Comanche
The Hopi
The Inuit
The Iroquois
The Mohawk
Native Americans of the Great Lakes
Native Americans of the Northeast
Native Americans of the Northwest Coast
Native Americans of the Northwest Plateau
Native Americans of the Plains
Native Americans of the Southeast
Native Americans of the Southwest
The Navajo
The Pawnee
Primary Sources
The Sioux

Indigenous Peoples of North America

# Native Americans of California

Stuart A. Kallen

San Diego • Detroit • New York • San Francisco • Cleveland • New Haven, Conn. • Waterville, Maine • London • Munich

*For more information, contact*
Lucent Books
27500 Drake Rd.
Farmington Hills, MI 48331-3535
Or you can visit our Internet site at http://www.gale.com



**LIBRARY OF CONGRESS CATALOGING-IN-PUBLICATION DATA**

Kallen, Stuart A., 1955–
Native Americans of California / by Stuart A. Kallen.
p. cm. — (Indigenous peoples of North America)
Summary: Discusses the cultural practices, religious beliefs, interaction with European settlers, and current lives of some of the native peoples of California.
Includes bibliographical references and index.
ISBN 1-59018-088-7 (hardback: alk. paper)
1. Indians of North America—California—Juvenile literature. [1. Indians of North America—California.] I. Title. II. Series.
E78 .C15 K36 2003
979.4'900497—dc21

2002152877

Printed in the United States of America

# Contents

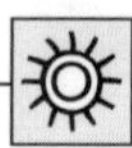

# Foreword

North America's native peoples are often relegated to history—viewed primarily as remnants of another era—or cast in the stereotypical images long found in popular entertainment and even literature. Efforts to characterize Native Americans typically result in idealized portrayals of spiritualists communing with nature or bigoted descriptions of savages incapable of living in civilized society. Lost in these unfortunate images is the rich variety of customs, beliefs, and values that comprised—and still comprise—many of North America's native populations.

The *Indigenous Peoples of North America* series strives to present a complex, realistic picture of the many and varied Native American cultures. Each book in the series offers historical perspectives as well as a view of contemporary life of individual tribes and tribes that share a common region. The series examines traditional family life, spirituality, interaction with other native and non-native peoples, warfare, and the ways the environment shaped the lives and cultures of North America's indigenous populations. Each book ends with a discussion of life today for the Native Americans of a given region or tribe.

In any discussion of the Native American experience, there are bound to be similarities. All tribes share a past filled with unceasing white expansion and resistance that led to more than four hundred years of conflict. One U.S. administration after another pursued this goal and fought Indians who attempted to defend their homelands and ways of life. Although no war was ever formally declared, the U.S. policy of conquest precluded any chance of white and Native American peoples living together peacefully. Between 1780 and 1890, Americans killed hundreds of thousands of Indians and wiped out whole tribes.

The Indians lost the fight for their land and ways of life, though not for lack of bravery, skill, or a sense of purpose. They simply could not contend with the overwhelming numbers of whites arriving from Europe or the superior weapons they brought with them. Lack of unity also contributed to the defeat of the Native Americans. For most, tribal identity was more important than racial identity. This loyalty left the Indians at a distinct disadvantage. Whites had a strong racial identity, and they fought alongside each other even when there was disagreement because they shared a racial destiny.

Although all Native Americans share this tragic history, they have many distinct differences. For example, some tribes and individuals sought to cooperate almost immediately with the U.S. government while others steadfastly resisted the white presence. Life before the arrival of white settlers also varied. The nomads of the Plains developed altogether different lifestyles and customs from the fishermen of the Northwest coast.

Contemporary life is no different in this regard. Many Native Americans—forced onto reservations by the American government—struggle with poverty, poor health, and inferior schooling. But others have regained a sense of pride in themselves and their heritage, enabling them to search out new routes to self-sufficiency and prosperity.

The *Indigenous Peoples of North America* series attempts to capture the differences as well as similarities that make up the experiences of North America's native populations—both past and present. Fully documented primary and secondary source quotations enliven the text. Sidebars highlight events, personalities, and traditions. Bibliographies provide readers with ideas for further research. In all, each book in this dynamic series provides students with a wealth of information as well as launching points for further research.

## Introduction

# The First Californians

California is a land of stunning natural wonders, from the golden sandy beaches of San Diego in the south to the magnificent coastal redwoods in the north. The snow-capped Sierra Nevada Mountains run through the center of the state, their granite hills fringed with towering sequoia trees over four thousand years old. The Great Basin region in the eastern part of California contains some of the world's harshest desert, including the high Mojave and the parched Death Valley.

California is also home to more than 30 million people, most of whom live in sprawling cities such as San Diego, Los Angeles, and the San Francisco Bay area. The once pristine mountains, beaches, and valleys of California are now filled with freeways, tract housing, strip malls, and glittering office buildings, most built within the last seventy-five years. In some areas the air is brown with pollution spewed from millions of cars and trucks that crawl across the roads in traffic jams every day.

Long before California became the land of highways and Hollywood, hundreds of thousands of Native Americans lived in the midst of its natural beauty. Unlike the white settlers who displaced them, the Indian tribes lived in harmony with their natural surroundings, taking what they could from the land to insure their survival.

There were about fifty tribes living in California, and these were divided into as many as five hundred bands, or tribelets. Some of the main tribes from north to south include the Yurok, Yuki, Shasta, Wintu, Maidu, Patwin, Pomo, Miwok, Ohlone, Yokuts, Monache, Chumash, Gabrielino, Cahuilla, Kumeyaay, and others. These peoples were separated from one another by rugged natural barriers such as mountains, canyons, and deserts, and each region supplied its native tribes with the necessary means of survival. With well-defined ancestral homelands there was little competition for food and territory and there were few conflicts between the tribes.

## Misunderstood Tribes

When Europeans began to arrive in California in large numbers in the eighteenth century, they were contemptuous of the Native Americans they met. In this land of plenty, the natives lived simply, wore almost no clothing, and owned few possessions. Like modern Californians, they preferred to spend most of their time outdoors. But the newcomers compared the natives unfavorably to the Aztecs, who built shimmering cities of turquoise and gold in Mexico, and the Iroquois, who created a complex agricultural society along the East Coast. This may be seen in the 1775 writings of Pedro Font, one of the early Spanish explorers in California. Font wrote that the Cahuilla tribe, who inhabited the region now called the Mojave, "are so savage, wild and dirty, disheveled, ugly, small and timid, that only because they have human form is it possible to believe that they belong to mankind."[1] Font, like most Europeans who came to the region, was hostile to the natives not only because of their physical appearance but because they were not Christians. Since at that time this attitude went almost completely unchallenged, the Europeans considered themselves to be justified in killing or enslaving California's original citizens and taking over their lands.

Today, however, it is clear that these Europeans failed to realize that the California tribes had a broad understanding of their natural surroundings. While they did not plant corn and beans like tribes did in the east, the natives tended the countryside as if it were a giant garden. They harvested wild grasses, seeds, acorns, roots, bulbs, and over five hundred other varieties of plants that they found hidden in the wilderness. These resources provided food, medicine, baskets, canoes, clothing, and shelter.

Prejudice kept the newcomers from appreciating the distinct cultures of the indigenous peoples, their deeply spiritual religious beliefs based on nature, and the intricate political alliances that had fostered peace in the region for a period far longer than Europeans had ever known. Tribespeople made everything they owned from natural materials, and while they did not have horses, metal, guns, or the wheel, they did exhibit a mastery of hunting, fishing, and other skills needed to thrive in the American West. These people were farmers, hunters, artisans, astronomers, weavers, poets, shamans, songwriters, healers, and more.

Since the tribes did not have a written language until they adopted Spanish or English, most of what has been written about them throughout the centuries was the work of white people, who often misunderstood or exaggerated aspects of their culture. In addition, when Native American religious beliefs and creation stories were written down for the first time, many were distorted to fit the Christian concepts of God and the devil.

Although the past several centuries have not been kind to the tribes of California,

Americans have come to terms with the native culture and the role white society played in its near destruction. A small percentage of Native American tribes have become associated with gambling casinos in some very highly visible areas around San Diego, Palm Springs, and elsewhere. For the first time in centuries, the tribes are amassing monetary and political capital. With this newfound wealth comes a renewal of pride. Despite centuries of actions that both unintentionally and intentionally were destructive of Native American culture, the first Americans have endured to preserve their heritage, tribal affinities, and distinctive religious beliefs.

Chapter 1

# Tribes of California

The Native Americans of California are descendents of ancient people called Paleo-Indians who first arrived in the area more than ten thousand years ago, near the end of the last Ice Age. These Paleo-Indians are believed to have migrated from Asia, having walked across the now sunken land bridge that once connected Russia's Siberia region with Alaska. The ancient people were nomads who followed large grass-eating herd animals such as bison, mammoth, and mastodon and hunted them with stone-tipped spears.

Around eight thousand years ago the climate warmed, and the mammoths and mastodons disappeared. The nomadic tribes were forced to cease their wandering and build semipermanent villages in areas where they could harvest wild seeds and plants to supplement their diet.

Researchers estimate that the population of Native Americans in California reached about three hundred thousand by the first century A.D., and a majority of the tribes were well settled into the regions where the European explorers found them fifteen centuries later.

Although California is populated by a number of diverse tribes, many share similar cultural features and languages that distinguish them from others. These divisions are often based on the natural features of the terrain that supported each tribe. Since they were completely dependent on the natural world to secure adequate food, tribes were affected by climate, topography, and available plants, animals, and water. These aspects in turn affected types of housing, tools, medicine, hunting and gathering methods, and even religious beliefs and practices.

## Tribes of Northwestern California

The northern coast of California is a cool, rainy environment where up to one hundred inches of rain can fall annually. In this rain forest setting, tribes such as the Shasta, Yurok, Tolowa, Hupa, Wiyot, and Karok (or Karuk) lived beneath ancient redwood

*Paleo-Indians spear a mammoth. Early Indians migrated across the Bering Strait into North America in pursuit of such large animals.*

trees that grew to a height of more than 350 feet. The great Klamath River, rich in salmon and other fish, flowed through this region, providing a constant source of food for the tribes. Almost everything the tribes needed could be found along the valleys of the Klamath River and its tributaries, and the riverbanks were dotted with dozens of Native American villages. The river was so important that tribes were named by their location on the water. For example, Yurok means "downriver people," since the tribes lived on the lower forty-five miles of the Klamath beginning at its delta at the Pacific Ocean. The Karok, conversely, were the "upriver people."

Culturally, the northwestern people were less like the Californians farther to the south and more like tribes to the north who lived in a similar rain forest environment in the area of present-day Oregon and Washington. Linguistically, the area around the Karok territory was a meeting of several ancient tongues. As Maureen Bell writes in *Karuk: The Upriver People:*

> [Within] a radius of six miles, three of the six major [Native American]

linguistic groups recognized in North America came into contact, sharing a similar culture. The Hupa, who spoke Athabascan, lived along the Trinity River south of the Karuk, while the Yurok . . . or Downriver People, who spoke Algonkian, resided on the Klamath just below and to the southwest of the Karuk. The ancient hunting grounds of the Tolowa were to the northwest. . . . The Shasta, who spoke a similar Hokan language to the Karuk lived to the east. . . . Despite linguistic differences, the most closely interrelated groups were the Karuk, Hupa, and Yurok—or the Klamath River Indians. Many of their laws, customs, and values were similar, and a large trade network existed between them. They also participated in each other's religious ceremonies and intermarried.[2]

## Land of Many Languages

In modern times California is a social melting pot where people of many cultures speak dozens of different languages. This was also true before the arrival of the white settlers, when Native Americans who lived in the region spoke a wide variety of unrelated languages.

The first known tribes to make their way into California spoke the Hokan, or Yuman, language, similar to that used by tribes such as the Yavapai in present-day Arizona. The next group of immigrants settled in the Central Valley and spoke a Penutian tongue similar to that of the Zunis in New Mexico. Around two thousand years ago, the last Native Americans to arrive were speakers of the Uto-Aztecan, or Shoshone, language, which also was spoken by tribes throughout a huge cross section of the Americas from southern Mexico to the East Coast of the United States. The Uto-Aztecan people came to California from the east and may have been pushed into the region by drought and food shortages in their homeland in the region of present-day Nevada and Utah.

Although they shared similar language groups, the isolated tribes spoke different variations that prevented them from communicating with one another. As James J. Rawls writes in *Indians of California:*

"Native California contained speakers of over one hundred dialects, 70 percent of which were as mutually unintelligible as English and Chinese. No area of comparable size in North America, or perhaps the world, contained a greater variety of native languages and cultures than did aboriginal California."

## Some Northern Coast Tribes

Farther south along the California coast, many tribes occupied the region between the Pacific Ocean and the North Coast Range, south of present-day Eureka to Marin County north of San Francisco Bay. With plentiful rainfall, this region is rich in diversity, with small patches of woodlands, grasslands, and chaparral located side by side. With abundant herbs, vegetables, and game it is little wonder that this was the most populated area of California, with tribes such as the Coast Yuki and Pomo living in the area.

*A Hupa woman of California's northwestern rain forest poses in native dress.*

The Yuki stood out in many ways. Unlike most other tribes, their language was not related to Hokan, Penutian, or other common Native American tongues. They also differed physically, being shorter and stockier than other California tribes. This is believed to have been a result of the isolated mountain region where they lived, as described by A.L. Kroeber in *Handbook of the Indians of California:* "Their country lies wholly in the Coastal Range mountains, which in this region are not . . . very high, but are much broken. They contain some valleys but the surface of the land in general is endlessly rugged."[3]

The Coast Yuki, however, lived in much more accessible territory along the rocky Mendocino coast and among the enormous redwoods that grow along what is now called the Russian River. About eleven tribelets made up the Coast Yuki, although their dialect of the Yuki language was mostly unintelligible to their relatives in the Coastal Range.

While the Coast Yuki occupied a small region, the tribelets that made up the Pomo ranged over a large area of what is now Sonoma, Lake, and southern Mendocino Counties. Although these tribespeople are collectively referred to as the Pomo tribe, Native Americans in this region were actually a conglomeration of bands that shared similar languages and customs. It was white settlers in the nineteenth century that grouped these people under one identity—Pomo—which was actually the name of an ancient village northwest of Ukiah. Similarly, the seven languages spoken by the tribes have been grouped together as dialects of the Pomo language.

Whatever the distinctions, the Pomo tribelets lived in a hospitable environment consisting of rocky Pacific shores, redwood-covered hillsides, the rich Russian River valley, and the shores of Clear Lake. Although rain and fog were common, these varied environments provided nearly every type of food source from seafood to elk.

## The Miwok

To the south, in what is now Sonoma and Marin Counties, the Miwok inhabited a similar environment. Reflecting their Penutian dialect, many Miwok names continue to grace the area: Olema means "lake"; Olompali, "south"; and Tamalpais, "coast hill." Place names along the northern California coast, such as Marin and Novato, are believed to have been named by the Spanish after Miwok chiefs.

Miwok territory is marked with extensive marshes, sloughs, lagoons, bays, and coastal terrain, which provided a rich buffet of food including crab, salmon, goose, bear, and more.

To the east, the Lake Miwok were isolated from their western relatives and surrounded by Pomo, Wintun, and Wappo at the southern end of Clear Lake. Farther east, more bands made up the tribe referred to as the Eastern Miwok. These tribelets occupied both sides of the Sacramento River north of present-day Stockton. Although these tribes may never have journeyed far enough west to see the ocean, they shared similar cultural traits with the Coast Miwok.

## Northeastern California

Like the northwestern tribes, the northeastern peoples lived in an environment reminiscent of Oregon and Washington. Here the peaks of the Cascade Mountains are covered with pine, Douglas fir, and juniper while the tableland of the Modoc Plateau is a dry environment dominated by sagebrush, wild grass, and scraggly western junipers. Thus tribes from this area had relatively few natural resources to ensure their survival. Fish were much less abundant, and these people ranged across great distances in the pursuit of game. Tribes were small and populations were densest along the valleys of the Fall and Pit Rivers, where the Achomawi and Atsugewi (sometimes called Pit River Indians) hunted migratory birds such as ducks and geese.

The Modoc, who lived in an approximately twenty-five-hundred-square-mile area on both sides of the Oregon-California border, depended on several lakes in the region, including Lower Klamath, Tule, Ness, Goose, and Clear Lakes, for survival. To the west, the permanently snowcapped peaks of 14,440-foot Mount Shasta provided a picturesque background to Modoc

villages. To the east, the Cascade Range could be seen rising above the trees. South of the Modoc homeland, the incredibly rugged landscape, now the Lava Beds National Monument, presented a forbidding area pocked with black cinder cones, lava flows, caves, and pit craters.

South of the lava beds, the timber and grasslands of the Sacramento River valley were home to the Wintu, Patwin, Maidu, and others. These tribes shared the Penutian language, although each tribelet spoke a different dialect. The Wintu was the most populous tribe in Northern California; they occupied a large region along the western banks of the Sacramento River into the foothills of the Sierras. The eastern banks of the river were home to the Yana and about one thousand members of the Maidu, who also made their homes in the natural wonderland of what is now Yosemite National Park. Maidu author Marie Potts, born in 1895, describes the region in *The Northern Maidu:*

> Our country was beautiful, with vast open valleys or meadows. . . . The surrounding mountains were covered with snow most of the year . . . and, looming above all, Mount Lassen where snow never completely melted. Among mountains and fine lakes . . . there was good fishing and plenty of deer roamed from valley to valley across ridges covered with sugar and ponderosa pine, fir, cedar, spruce, and tamaracks. . . . There were all kinds of berry bushes on both meadows and hillsides; raspberries, strawberries, elderberries, gooseberries . . . and, of course, there were huckleberries. . . . Our country was rich in nature's food for the taking.[4]

## The Bay Area

Like their northern brethren, tribes of central California inhabited a widely diverse environment from the San Francisco Bay area across the coastal ranges, through the San Joaquin Valley, and onto the Sierra Nevada. Then as now, this region contained some of the most incredibly beautiful natural scenery found anywhere in the world.

Life was extremely satisfying for the ten to twenty thousand members of the Ohlone tribe that lived in the area between present-day San Francisco Bay and Big Sur. Composed of forty associated tribelets—each with about 250 members—the Ohlone spoke twelve different dialects of the Penutian language. And linguists estimate that each dialect averaged only one thousand speakers. This fact startled the Spanish when they arrived in the eighteenth century, as Malcolm Margolin writes in *The Ohlone Way*: "That so many independent groups of people speaking so many different languages could be packed into such a relatively small area boggled the European mind."[5]

While over ten million people reside in the bay area today, in the days of the Ohlone it was a spectacular wilderness. The bay, along with the rivers, lakes, wetlands, and streams, attracted an infinite variety of wildlife. Massive flocks of geese, ducks, cormorants, pelicans, and other birds darkened the sky. Rocks and ledges along the clean, clear ocean waters were covered by hundreds of thousands of seals while the ocean was littered with a profusion of mussels, abalone, oysters, lobsters, and other sea creatures. These washed ashore attracting legions of grizzly bears who gorged on the remains.

## The Yokuts of the Central Valley

The coast was not the only place of abundance for California's Native American tribes. Inland, in the fertile, 350-mile-long

## The Kawaiisu of Tehachapi

The Kawaiisu lived in the Tehachapi Mountains, which skirt the bottom of the Central Valley, and traded with the other tribes that surrounded their homeland. The following information about the Kawaiisu is taken from the article "Kawaiisu Culture" found on the *bakersfield.com* website:

"All native groups of the region had knowledge of resources to be found in the area. This suggests a well-developed system of family relationships through intermarriage. Frequent visits ensured a continual flow of food stuffs and other goods. Out of these visits grew a system of trails which led in all directions from the core area. The trail system was used to make contact with the Paiute of the Owens Valley, the Koso of the Panamint range [in Death Valley], the Chemehuevi of the eastern Mojave desert and the Yokuts of the San Joaquin Valley. One trail led west and resulted in contact with the Chumash of the central coast. Another headed north to the homelands of the Tubatulabal along the Kern River. An important trail took them north to what is now Walker Pass, facilitating contact with the Koso; a branch of this trail led to Red Rock Canyon [in Kern County]."

Central Valley where the San Joaquin River flows, about seventy thousand Yokuts, or *Yoh' coots*, created a thriving society.

The Yokuts were made up of about fifty separate tribelets that inhabited a broad swath of California's heartland. They occupied more territory than any other California tribe, spreading out over approximately one-third of the state, from the confluence of the Sacramento and San Joaquin Rivers in the north to the Tehachapi Mountains south of Bakersfield. Within this vast territory—estimated at thirteen thousand square miles—the Yokuts lived along the banks and canyons of nearly every major river including the Fresno, Kern, King, Merced, and Stanislaus.

These tribelets probably never traveled more than fifteen or twenty miles from their native regions, and so developed distinctive dialects of their native language. In fact, the fifty tribes spoke fifty different jargons and, as A.L. Kroeber writes, "Such an array of dialects is unparalleled, and gives to the Yokuts alone nearly one-third of all the different forms of speech talked in the State. The different languages from tribe to tribe were often rather limited; but they are marked enough to be readily perceptible to the interested Caucasian observer."[6] The twenty tribes of the Northern

Valley Yokuts lived in a region between the present-day city of Stockton in the north and the Fresno River in the south.

The thirty-one thousand people that made up the fifteen tribelets of the Southern Valley Yokuts lived in the upper end of the San Joaquin Valley between Fresno and the Tehachapis for at least eight thousand years. Tribes in this region experienced short, mild winters, long, hot summers with temperatures topping one hundred degrees Fahrenheit, and rainfall of only five to ten inches annually. However, rivers and river-fed lakes such as the Buena Vista, Kern, and Tulare prevented the area from becoming a complete desert. These bodies of water also supported numerous swamps, marshes, and sloughs that attracted a wide and diverse array of wildlife.

## The Monache of the Great Basin

While the Yokuts inhabited a large portion of central California, their neighbors to the east, the Monache, or Western Mono, were related to the Paiute tribes of the Great Basin region of Nevada and Utah.

*The Monache migrated across the High Sierras and settled among the sequoias (foreground) of the lower elevations of the Sierra Nevada mountain range.*

The Monache were actually made up of six separate but related tribes who, around A.D. 1350, crossed over the lofty great divide of the High Sierras from their ancestral homeland in the east. These people did not speak Penutian as their Yokuts neighbors did but, instead, shared the Numic language with the Paiutes.

The Monache lived in some of the most breathtaking wilderness in the world, in the remote and isolated valleys around what is now Sequoia National Park. And the beautiful mountains covered with ancient sequoia trees offered many advantages to the Monache, such as numerous rabbits, squirrels, elk, deer, and antelope, and streams that ran thick with fish. In the spring the hills exploded with a rainbow of wildflowers including purple lupine, Indian paintbrush, and California poppies.

## The Chumash of Southern California

West of the Monache lands, approximately seventeen thousand members of the Chumash tribes inhabited a broad section of the California coast from Point Conception south to Malibu, or *Maliwu,* as the Chumash village was called. The Chumash were also a maritime people who sailed the ocean in canoes and settled on Santa Cruz, Santa Rosa, and San Miguel Islands south of Santa Barbara. Today the region, with cities such as Santa Barbara and Ventura, has one of the best climates and is one of the most desirable places to live in the United States. This was also true when the Chumash resided there, as A.L. Kroeber writes:

> Marine life along the Chumash shores is exceptionally rich, the climate far famed, and every condition favored the unusual concentration of population among a people living directly upon nature. The land, however, is dry; the watercourses, though long, are small and rarely run permanently, and each successive mountain chain increases the aridity. Only some narrow stretches among the uplands of the western end of the Tehachapi range are more favorable. There was thus every occasion for the inlander to drift to the edge of the ocean, if he could, but small inducement for the coast people to go to the interior, except for occasional visits. The population in the districts away from the sea must have been comparatively light.[7]

The Chumash had at least six distinct dialects of their language, from regions such as Ventura, Santa Barbara, and so on. The tribes referred to the people who lived on the Santa Cruz Islands as *Michumash*, or "island people." When the Spanish arrived, they corrupted this word into Chumash, and the mainland tribes have borne this inaccurate label ever since.

## The Powerful Gabrielino

The Chumash shared the southernmost reaches of their territory with the Gabrielino tribe whose five to ten thousand members once inhabited all of pre-

## Chumash History

The Chumash had a long and illustrious history in one of America's most beautiful regions, as Eugene N. Anderson Jr. writes in *The Chumash Indians of Southern California:*

"The Chumash, over thousands of years, had achieved greater and greater success in wresting a livelihood from their territory in modern Ventura, Santa Barbara, and San Luis Obispo counties. Their history since the coming of the white man has been one of steady decline.

Indians have occupied the coasts and islands of Southern California for ten thousand years or more. Whether the Chumash entered the area early or late is not known, but archeology shows no drastic changes in their lifeway during at least the most recent centuries. The Chumash language, although related to many languages of central and northern California, is highly distinctive, and has been separate from other tongues for thousands of years. The origins of the Chumash are thus shrouded in the mystery that covers so many ancient events in Californian prehistory.

When Juan Rodriguez Cabrillo, in 1542, made the first exploration of the California coast, he spent much time with the Chumash. He died in Chumash territory on San Miguel Island, south of the Santa Barbara mainland. He saw them as a flourishing, numerous, good-looking people, living in villages large enough to be called towns, and possessing plank canoes and other sophisticated items of manufacture. Subsequent explorers . . . found Chumash life unchanged and undisturbed. Then, from 1769 through 1776, several Spanish expeditions passed through California. . . . In 1782, came the first permanent white settlement in Chumash territory, the mission of Santa Barbara."

sent-day Los Angeles County and the northern half of Orange County from Topanga Canyon to Laguna Beach. Like the Chumash, the Gabrielino were also maritime people, inhabiting San Clemente, San Nicholas, and Catalina Islands. But the tribe was given their name by the Spanish because they lived near the San Gabriel Mission and the San Gabriel Mountains.

Just as the people in this region today are some of the richest in the United States, the Gabrielino were considered the wealthiest and most powerful tribe in Southern California. This is in part because of the abundance of food that grew naturally within the mountains and foothills, the coastal prairie, and coastal regions that made up their homeland. As A.L. Kroeber writes:

> The Gabrielino occupied the greatest bulk of the most fertile lowland portion of southern California. They occupied also a stretch of pleasant and sheltered coast and the most favored one of the Santa Barbara Islands. They seem to have been the most advanced group south of Tehachapi. . . . They certainly were the wealthiest . . . and dominated [other tribes] wherever contacts occurred.[8]

The Gabrielino tribe members adapted to several distinctly different regions within the Los Angeles basin. In addition to the islands, they lived in ecological zones such as coastal marshes, grasslands, oak woodlands, interior mountains, exposed coast, sheltered coast, and chaparral. Each zone determined the diet of the tribes. For example, in exposed coast regions, the Gabrielino were able to harvest a wide array of seafood, while in coastal marshes, people depended on waterfowl, frogs, snakes, and other aquatic animals.

## The Luiseño

Like the Gabrielino, the four thousand members of the Luiseño tribe had no formal name for themselves but were named by the Spanish. In this case, the tribal name is derived from the fact that the Luiseño lived near the site of the Mission San Luis Rey, built in 1798.

The Luiseño lived in a much wider region than the area around Mission San Luis Rey. In fact, they inhabited the area that today includes the southern half of Orange County down to Oceanside in San Diego County. The tribe also ranged inland to the first high ridge of coastal mountains such as Santiago Peak and 6,138-foot Palomar Mountain. Robert F. Heizer describes their environment in *California*, vol. 8 of *Handbook of North American Indians:* "[The Luiseño lands] covered every ecological zone from the ocean, sandy beaches, shallow inlets, marshes, coastal chaparral, lush interior grass valleys, extensive groves, up to the pines and cedars on the top of Mount Palomar."[9]

## The Cahuilla of the Desert

The favorable living conditions in Luiseño lands were out of reach for the Cahuilla tribes living to the east in some of the harshest terrain in the world. But the Cahuilla were relative latecomers to Southern California, having arrived about two to three thousand years ago, long after the best lands along the coast were settled by the Luiseño, Gabrielino, Chumash, and others.

The Cahuilla occupied the rocky canyons, tall mountains, steep-sided valleys, and hot, dry desert of southeastern California. This starkly beautiful region contains few forests or lush, green plants. Instead it is the territory of the palm tree, mesquite bush, cactus, yucca, and other desert vegetation. But, like many other parts of California, the region also contains several distinct environmental zones. For example, the Cahuilla lived near the 11,000-foot San Bernardino mountain peaks as well as in the Salton Sink, which

*The Luiseño are named after Mission San Luis Rey de Francia (pictured), second of the twenty-one Spanish missions built along El Camino Real.*

is 273 feet *below* sea level. Temperatures in these areas may soar up to 125 degrees Fahrenheit in the summer with rainfall a paltry 3.5 inches annually—less than what might fall in a few days around the San Francisco Bay area.

This sort of varied climate kept some Cahuilla moving from place to place, traveling in the desert during the warm winters and moving to the mountains during the hot summers. In addition, the Cahuilla were on generally friendly terms with the coastal tribes such as the Luiseño and Gabrielino, and so might walk to the seashore to escape the summer heat.

## The Kumeyaay

Like the Cahuilla, the Kumeyaay of San Diego and Imperial Counties and northern Baja California, Mexico, were probably later arrivals in California, having moved to the area around fifteen hundred years ago. And the culture and language of the Kumeyaay has more in common with the tribes of Arizona and New Mexico than it does with the Luiseño and Gabrielino.

The Kumeyaay were originally two tribes called the Tipai and the Ipai, but the Spanish renamed them both the Diegueños, after the Mission San Diego de Alcalá. In the 1970s the collective tribes of Yuman-speaking Indians in the region coined the name *Kumeyaay*, the term that is used today.

The Kumeyaay hunted and gathered along the San Diego coast down into the area of present-day Ensenada, Mexico. The tribe also ranged far inland past the tall peaks of the Cuyamaca and Laguna Mountains and beyond the Salton Sink to the Arizona border. This region contained everything from the idyllic temperatures found along the Southern California coast to the nearly unbearable heat in the Colorado desert. Within these broad ecological zones, specific areas could be extremely supportive of human habitation. While the coastal wetlands were obviously attractive places to site villages, freshwater springs in the desert also attracted Kumeyaay tribelets.

*Sitting in the shade of a cluster of palm trees, a Cahuilla woman displays a large basket used for gathering and storing food.*

## Thousands of Years of History

The Kumeyaay, Ohlone, Chumash, and others are but a few of the fifty or so tribes that once occupied California. Each played a significant role in their specific region, and all were important in their own right. In a land of abundance, these Native American tribes enjoyed thousands of years of peace and prosperity. They developed remarkable cultures and invented ingenious ways to live in harmony with nature. California has often been referred to as Heaven on Earth. For the Native Americans who lived in its groves, canyons, bays, and seashores, paradise was an everyday reality for more than eight hundred centuries.

## Chapter 2

# Village Life in Southern California

With its abundance of mountains, grasslands, deserts, and beaches there are few places on Earth as rich in plant and animal resources as California. And those gifts from nature were ingeniously utilized by Native American tribes to sustain themselves for more than eight thousand years.

With survival essentially guaranteed, tribal life revolved around the study of nature; the tribes of California possessed a keen understanding of nearly every plant and animal that thrived in their homeland. When Europeans first arrived, they described places such as the Colorado River valley as barren, dead, and lifeless. But members of the Cahuilla tribe who called that place home saw food in the mesquite bean, water in the tiny seeps beneath the parched ground, and clothing and shelter in the wild grasses that grew in the shade. And the Cahuilla lived in one of the harshest climates on earth.

### Villages in the North

Like the Cahuilla, the lives of California's other tribes were dominated by the natural environment that surrounded them. In the northwest, towering redwoods provided strong, durable wood for many uses. The Tolowa, Yurok, and others utilized redwood planks to build sturdy structures, called family houses, to protect them from the rain.

Before work could begin, a tall redwood tree had to be felled without the benefit of saws or axes. Instead, the tribesmen built a hot fire at the base of a large redwood, stoking the flames until, days later, the tree finally toppled. Planks were cut by wedges fashioned from elk antlers that were pounded into the straight-grained redwoods with stone hammers. Scrapers made from sharpened mussel shells smoothed the wood into planks that, although they were ragged and uneven, were quite useful for construction.

When building a house, tribesmen excavated a hole about three feet deep and ten feet square. Upright redwood planks about six feet high were set around the pit and lashed together with grapevine. The roof was pitched in the middle, or sometimes in several places, to deflect rain. A roof hole allowed smoke to escape from the central fire pit inside the dwelling, and this hole could be closed off with a board during storms. People entered and exited the home by way of a hole about two feet in diameter, cut a few inches above the ground. Inside, a ladder aided the descent into the living area. Outside the entryway, a porch made from flat river stones served as a patio on sunny days and starlit nights.

Each small home fulfilled several roles, serving as shelter, bedroom, storage space, workshop, and kitchen. A.L. Kroeber describes the interior of one such Yurok dwelling: "The hard earth floor is generally swept fairly clean, but most Yurok [homes] are untidy, and cooked food, eatables in preparation, unfinished baskets, materials, implements temporarily laid aside, and a variety of apparatus litter the cramped space, while from above half-cured slabs of salmon may drip grease, or gusts of rain drift in."[10]

These family houses were occupied by a man's wives, unmarried daughters, and infant sons. Men and boys who had reached puberty lived together in sweat lodges where, in addition to taking sweat baths,

*Pictured is a typical Hupa sweat lodge, where the men and adolescent boys of the tribe lived and interacted with one another.*

*Bay Area tribes lived in huts of woven mats of tule reeds held together with pieces of willow.*

tribesmen made tools, swapped stories, and gambled.

In the eastern part of the state, the Modoc built winter lodges in about twenty-one separate villages. These homes were circular and large, up to forty feet in diameter, and had to withstand frigid temperatures and snowdrifts that could pile up to six feet high. Four large upright trees were used to hold support beams for the roof. Wood rafters were placed over this framework, and mats of tule, a plentiful marsh grass, were layered on the wood. This foundation was buried under twelve inches of earth that had previously been removed from the pit. A central hole acted as a doorway and smoke vent. Inside, the floor was covered with soft grasses, and bearskin beds lay on the floor along the outer walls.

Sweat lodges also played an important role for the Modoc and were used by both men and women. These buildings doubled as community centers for prayers and other religious activities.

## Villages of the Bay Area

California's coastal strip from present-day San Francisco down through Big Sur was the land of the Ohlone, Esselen, and Salinan tribes. Within the bountiful bay area, the Ohlone flourished and multiplied, making this region one of the most populated on the West Coast. Before the arrival of the Spanish, about forty permanent villages ringed the river deltas, cliffs, rocky shores, wetlands, and sandy beaches that surrounded San Francisco Bay. Each village averaged about two hundred people, although populations of fifty to five hundred were found at various sites.

Tribespeople lived in small domed houses constructed from mats made of thatched tule reeds, alfalfa, and ferns. These mats were attached by tough, supple pieces of willow, called withes, to a framework of willow poles pounded upright into the ground and angled inward to meet at a central point. Houses were about six to twenty feet in diameter, and the

## An Ohlone Village Scene

In *The Ohlone Way* Malcolm Margolin recreates a typical day in an Ohlone village:

"The village is located along the eastern shores of the San Francisco Bay at the mouth of a freshwater creek. An immense, sprawling pile of shells, earth, and ashes elevates the site above the surrounding marshland. On top of this mound stand some fifteen dome-shaped tule houses arranged around a plaza-like clearing. Scattered among them are smaller structures that look like huge baskets on stilts—granaries in which the year's supply of acorns are stored. Beyond the houses and granaries lies another cleared area that serves as a ball field, although it is not now in use.

It is mid-afternoon of a clear, warm day. In several places throughout the village steam is rising from underground pit ovens where mussels, clams, rabbit meat, fish, and various roots are being roasted for the evening meal. People are clustered near the doors of the houses. Three men sit together, repairing a fishing net. A group of children are playing an Ohlone version of hide-and-seek: one child hides and all the rest are seekers. Here and there an older person is lying face down on a woven tule mat, napping in the warmth of the afternoon sun."

*A contemporary Native American repairs his fishing net.*

larger huts could accommodate several families, up to a dozen people.

To enter a tule hut, people crawled on their hands and knees through small rectangular doorways. Inside the home, a fire pit dominated the center of the space; and according to Malcolm Margolin, nearly every other item used for Ohlone survival was stored throughout the hut:

> [Each] house is crowded with possessions. Blankets of deer skin, bear skin, and woven rabbit skin lie strewn about the central fire pit. Hamper baskets in which seeds, roots, dried meat, and dried fish are stored stand against the smoke-darkened walls. . . . Tucked into rafters are bundles of basket-making material, plus deer-skin pouches that contain ornaments and tools; sets of awls, bone scrapers, file stones, obsidian knives, and twist drills for making holes in beads. Many of the houses also contain ducks stuffed with tule (to be used as hunting decoys), piles of fishing nets, fish traps, snares, clay balls ready to be ground into paint, and heaps of abalone shells that . . . will eventually be traded eastward for pine nuts, everyone hopes.[11]

Tribal chiefs had the largest houses because they were expected to entertain guests and needed more room to store food and gifts.

In addition to their tule huts, villagers constructed a number of other buildings. Men and women gathered in sweat lodges that were simply caves dug into the banks of streams. These saunas could hold six to eight people and were used for spiritual purposes and also to work in. Men carved arrowheads and tools while in the sweats while others played flutes and rhythm sticks as accompaniment.

Back in the village, tribes constructed domed community buildings large enough to hold up to two hundred people. These huts were used for meetings and dances. After several years, all of these buildings made from organic materials became infested with fleas and other vermin. At that time, the residents simply burned them and started anew.

In addition to the permanent villages, Native Americans from throughout the bay area built dozens of temporary camps, used only for a few months a year when the tribes journeyed to specific regions to fish and collect seafood. Building sites were determined by access to the shore, availability of timber and fresh water, and shelter from the wind. When living in these temporary camps, tribespeople feasted on mussels, oysters, and other shellfish, and left behind huge piles of shells, some up to one mile long and twenty feet deep. As Malcolm Margolin writes: "At the turn of [the twentieth century] more than 400 shellmounds, the remains of these villages and camps, could still be found along the shores of the Bay—dramatic indication of a thriving population."[12]

## South Coast Villages

Like the Ohlone, the Chumash lived in permanent villages where homes were constructed of tule grass. Since fresh water

## Sweat Lodges and Hunting

California tribes hunted deer and other animals with bows and arrows. Kills were often made at close range, and hunters had to make sure that their human scent did not scare off the prey. In *Handbook of Yokuts Indians*, originally published in 1949, Frank F. Latta describes the importance of sweat lodges in the hunting process:

"The sweat house was held in high esteem by all Indians. . . . Most Indian hunting was done by stalking and calling. Deer and other animals were killed with bow and arrow, probably always at a distance of less than thirty feet. . . . It readily is appreciated that often at a distance of several hundred yards, deer will scent a hunter and take flight. The Indian knew this. For this reason, he was very careful about several things. Always his hunting equipment was hung where it would not be touched except when he went hunting. In this way, it carried no human scent.

Before going hunting, and wearing all of his clothing, the Indian sweated [in a sweat lodge] and after sweating bathed in the river. Taking down his weapons, he proceeded to the game country with the knowledge that, for at least five or six hours, deer and other game would not be able to distinguish his scent. As this use gave the sweat house a very practical, even a vital function, it is not strange that the Indians . . . almost universally came to regard it as possessed of supernatural power and, because of this, sacred."

was important in this arid climate, the villages were usually constructed near water sources such as lakes, rivers, and streams. Other factors, such as good beaches for launching canoes, were also taken into consideration.

Chumash territory contained hundreds of villages, some large, some small. The biggest ones, around the Santa Barbara Channel, acted as centers for trade and politics for the entire Chumash region.

Chumash villages had features similar to those of the northern coast tribes, but put to slightly different uses. For example, the Chumash also had sweat lodges, called *temescales*, but theirs were built underground with mud and thatch roofs. Access was by way of a ladder through a hole in the roof. Chumash sweat lodges were used mainly by men about to go deer hunting. Before this important task, the men threw various fragrant herbs on the steaming rocks to mask their human odor, which would have scared off deer and other game.

Central to Chumash villages were community huts, known as *siliyik*, where sacred dances were performed. These semicircular buildings were open on one side so spectators could watch shamans perform rituals inside. The Chumash also set aside special areas for production activities where men could chip tools from stone, construct canoes from tule reeds, and work with beads.

## San Joaquin Villages

Like all Southern California tribes, the Yokuts also utilized tule grass in home construction. But when the Spanish first arrived in the San Joaquin Valley, which they named after Saint Joachim, they reported that the Indians came running out of underground burrows like rabbits. These visitors were unaware that the Yokuts did not live in holes but had designed for themselves comfortable earth-sheltered homes that offered insulation from the hot summer sun and protection from the cool rains of winter.

The Yokuts built their homes along lake or river shores where great quantities of tule and brush could be found. During construction they dug neat round holes in the earth, using sticks to loosen the dirt and baskets to remove the debris that was piled up nearby. For single family homes, the pit might be twelve feet in diameter, while large multifamily homes might require a pit one hundred feet across.

Willow poles were pounded upright around the two-foot-deep hole, and other sticks were woven around them to create a dome that resembled an upside-down wicker basket. After a thatch of tule was attached to the frame, the dirt that had been excavated was wetted, applied in a four-foot-thick layer, and beaten down with sticks. Within months of construction, grass and other plants began to grow on these earth homes, and when visitors such as the Spanish approached, it appeared as if the Yokuts villagers were simply emerging from underground.

As remarkable as the earth homes were, the Yokuts also constructed communal multifamily houses, called *kawe*, from willow poles and tule mats. These dramatic structures, shaped like elongated pup tents, could be three hundred feet in length and hold an entire village. Inside, each family had its own space—its own door, and its own smoky fireplace. Along the walls were beds made from tule mats topped with warm, comfortable bearskins. A profusion of food and personal goods such as dried meats, clothing, and bows and arrows, hung from the rafters. Thomas A. Baker, who founded the city of Bakersfield, described one such lodge in 1863: "[There] were strings of acorns and dried fish hanging from the pole framework. There were also baskets and bags of all kinds of Indians things on the ground inside. Everything was so smoked up inside that you couldn't tell what most of it was."[13] Baker must have visited the Yokuts lodge in the winter, because the tribes usually cooked outdoors, weather permitting.

## Mountain Villages

Up from the valley floor, the Foothill Yokuts constructed cone-shaped shelters about twelve to fifteen feet in diameter with a framework of poles held together in the middle with large willow hoops. A smoke hole was left in the center, and the frame was covered with pine bark, pine needles, or whatever local materials were available.

Sweat lodges were built of heavy oak timbers covered with brush and mud. Anthropologist Robert F. G. Spier describes the function of a typical sweat:

> Foothills Yokuts sweathouses used only the heat of the fire; no heated stones or steam was employed. The men, with women and children excluded, sat close along the walls and talked or sang while they sweated. Each sweat was followed by a plunge into a nearby pool or stream.
>
> The sweathouses [when not used for this primary purpose], were warm places to relax in cold winter weather. Women evidently went into the houses for this purpose when no men were around. . . . Men and boys might sleep in the sweathouse when quarters were crowded at home. Young, single men regularly stayed at the sweathouses.[14]

## Makeup and Tattoos

Like some modern Californians, tribes of the south coast used potions to prevent sunburn and enjoyed face makeup and even tattoos, as Bernice Eastman Johnston writes in *California's Gabrielino Indians:*

"In appearance these people were not tall, but stocky, muscular, and well-fleshed. Their skin was not as dark as that of certain other California tribes, but a soft, warm brown, even rather fair in childhood. A report to this effect made by the [sixteenth century explorer Juan] Cabrillo expedition of Catalina Islanders gave rise to some fantastic notions of a special race of "white Indians" being found there at that time. The women postponed the browning and wrinkling effect of the weather as long as possible with the liberal use of red ochre paint, but the girls used this more tastefully, as rouge, with an eye to vanity. Both men and women fancied tattooing on the forehead, the women sometimes preferring a decoration of the chin and sometimes an area from the eyes down to the breast. The skin was pricked with a thorn or a tiny fragment of flint, whereupon charcoal from the yucca cabbage, called in Spanish "mescal," or the juice of nightshade leaves, was rubbed into the small, bleeding wounds, making a strong blue-black tattoo. The young girls were tattooed before puberty."

*Sweat houses like this one were used by California Indians as a place to live, relax, and interact with other members of the tribe.*

Further up in the Sierras, the men, women, and children of the Monache tribes used the community sweat house in a similar manner. They also constructed conical, bark-covered houses but did not reside in large organized villages. Instead, the Monache had small hamlets consisting of five to twenty people residing in one to eight huts. Within these hamlets, huts would be set in a semicircle with the home of the chief located at the center.

## Desert Villages

Life in the desert required that the Cahuilla take weather patterns into consideration in the siting of their villages. As a result, they chose locations in canyons where cool winds blew down from higher elevations in the summer and warm breezes blew up-canyon in the winter.

Like their neighbors to the north, Cahuilla tribe members built houses from tule, but they also utilized palm fronds, mesquite branches, and other local desert plants. In Cahuilla villages family members might construct two or three such shelters and connect them with roofed walkways and walled windbreaks, called ramadas, where people could perform domestic chores.

## Water, Quakes, and Fire

In the searing desert, the Cahuilla depended on water from lakes, rivers, streams, springs, seeps, and marshy pools for survival. In some years, rain and melting mountain snow was abundant, and such bodies of water ran clean and fresh. In drought years, however, tribes could be severely stressed by lack of water. One way to alleviate this problem was to dig large holes in the ground to collect droplets of water that oozed out of the desert floor. In *The Cahuilla Indians* Harry C. James comments on this ingenious adaptation to local conditions: "These wells were unique in both conception and in execution. So far as we know, no other tribe of North American Indians ever dug wells. Wherever there was a feeble spring or a seep the Desert Cahuilla, with great labor, would construct a long, narrow, open passageway to it, often with steps at the end down to the water."[15]

While the Cahuilla could deal with the occasional drought, earthquakes, so common in Southern California, created unpredictable and often unpleasant situations. Cahuilla tribesman Francisco Patencio recounts one ancient lesson:

> One time . . . there came such earthquakes as had not been known to any of the people. Whole mountains

*Indians who lived in hot, dry areas built windbreaks and roofed walkways called ramadas to shelter themselves from the wind and sun.*

split—some rose up where there had been none before. Other peaks went down, and never came up again. It was a terrible time. The mountains that the people knew well were strange places that they had never seen before.

Then it was that Tahquitz Creek went dry, and only ran water in the winter time, and other streams that ran good water all year around have only been winter streams since. And so the Indians could not raise crops on that mesquite land any more. The climate seemed to change. The Andreas Canyon Creek that only ran in the winter became an all year stream, as it has been since. Before the earthquakes, the only water to be had there in the summer months was from a small spring which ran always in the creek beneath the caves. There were many springs on the mountain sides and on the level land. When the rains came less, they dried out and went away. No one knows where they used to be any more.[16]

While major earthquakes were rare, the Cahuilla faced other natural disasters on a regular basis. Wildfires caused by light-

*The desert-dwelling Cahuilla built their three-sided huts with grasses lashed to poles, placing the fourth wall in front of the dwelling as a windbreak.*

ning and human carelessness could spread and quickly engulf villages. Shelters made from dried grass and palm leaves could ignite in a matter of seconds. Fires could wipe out thousands of acres of plant vegetation the Cahuilla depended on for food, while also killing game animals. After wildfires, winter rains would sweep down the denuded hills much faster, causing flash floods and mud slides.

## Kumeyaay Campsites

In the southwestern regions of California occupied by the Kumeyaay, earthquakes, fires, and floods were an occasional problem. But in this idyllic climate the tribes barely needed shelters or villages to protect them from heat and cold. Instead, the Kumeyaay were seminomadic, moving to various campsites as they migrated from the mountains in the summer to the beaches in the winter.

Summer structures might consist only of a palm-frond lean-to or a windbreak propped between several shade trees. In winter, the tribe members might construct reed huts over slightly sunken floors or live in shallow caves. Those living in sloughs or near the beach constructed thatch and pole buildings and covered them with sand. As Michael Baksh writes in "The Kumeyaay" on the *Daphne* website:

> Although clans moved from place to place within their general territory, some locations were occupied for longer periods and by more people than others. . . . These settlements, which may be regarded as villages, were places to which the people returned from their foraging, where they spent winter months, sometimes in association with other clans. . . . Some larger groups appear to have had sizable summer as well as winter villages. . . . Within each village there was a dance floor, extensive milling stations, family living areas, and possibly a sweathouse and granary. If it was a winter camp, a house would have been set directly on the ground and a fireplace built on the ground by the door. . . . The Kumeyaay did not make summer houses. . . . Instead, the summer village needed only a windbreak, trees, or a cave fronted with rocks.[17]

## Village Politics

In every California tribe there was a chief or sachem to oversee village policy and politics. But chiefs were not expected to act as leaders in the American sense. According to Malcolm Margolin:

> Among the . . . Yokuts, Ohlones, and other California people the chief was not seen as someone who would energetically lead the people to a new or better way of life. The better way of life lay in the past. The goal of the chief was not to lead at all, certainly not to innovate, but rather to maintain the ancient . . . balances—the balances within the tribelet, between the tribelet and its neighbors, and between the tribelet and

its gods. The chief was expected to keep these ancient balances so that life would stay very much the same as it had been since time immemorial.[18]

People valued this service to such a degree that they often showered the chief and his family with gifts. In addition to having the largest house in the village, the chief had the most wives and many large baskets overflowing with food, clothing, and household goods. The chief also reserved the right to be the first to trade with strangers. But he was not expected to take advantage of his situation. His possessions were considered part of the entire village's wealth that could be distributed to anyone in need, including the sick, the old, the infirm, and the destitute. And, as Malcolm Margolin writes, "if anyone in the community was homeless or hungry, the chief would have been thoroughly disgraced, both in his own eyes and in the eyes of his people."[19]

*A chief of the Klamath tribe poses in full ceremonial regalia. Indian chiefs were expected to maintain balance within the tribe.*

Each village had its own chief, but no one person ruled over all the related tribelets. In small villages where nearly everyone was related, the chief was simply the family elder. But each group of tribelets usually had one village that was considered the center of trade and ceremony, and the chief of this place was considered the most important, since the vital business of the tribe was conducted here.

The position of chief was hereditary—handed down from father to son. Tribal chiefs could often trace their lineage back dozens of generations. But when an old chief died, his sons, or sometimes other relatives, would jockey for position. During this time the heads of all tribelet families came together, along with leading traders and holy men, to pick the new chief. Usually they picked the eldest son, but if there was no son, or he was deemed unfit, the men might pick a daughter, brother, or nephew. The only unbroken rule was that the new chief had to be a member of the old chief's close family.

The chief depended on these advisers, and considered them assistants. Some were in charge of running festivals, ceremonies, and gatherings. Others acted as messengers, spreading a chief's decisions throughout the village. Additional assistants included doctors, astronomers, singers, and storytellers.

The chief and his assistants were among the upper classes of his people, along with canoe builders, craftsmen, priests, and other specialists. Below this group, which made up about 25 percent of the average tribe, were the middle classes. These were the average people who were hunters, gatherers, fishermen, and other workers. On the bottom of society were the lowest classes—the lazy, the dishonest, and the rebellious ones who bucked society's dictates. And in the California land of plenty the Native Americans in these groups functioned in complex, diverse societies unlike those anywhere on earth.

## Chapter 3

# A Land of Plenty

When the Europeans first came to North America, they noticed that Native American women on the East Coast were farmers who, over the centuries, had learned to cultivate corn, beans, squash, tobacco, and other crops. Tribes in Southern California, however, did not need to farm the land in order to accumulate enough food to survive. Instead, they relied on hundreds of species of fish, game, and edible plants that nature generously provided year round.

While the California tribes were not technically farmers, they were stewards of the land. They encouraged the growth of favored plants by managing controlled burns that killed weeds, eliminated harmful insects, and fertilized the soil. Women also weeded certain areas to promote the growth of preferred vegetation and diverted streams to irrigate areas where plants grew naturally.

Partially as a result of their intelligent observation of the environment, California tribes had the most varied diets of any tribes in North America. Some collected shellfish along the ocean; others fished for salmon in rivers and lakes. Most were hunters of mammals, from seals on the coast to snakes and mice in the desert. And all gathered roots, herbs, bulbs, and all other manner of plant life. Whatever else they ate, all California tribes could depend on several staples that never seemed to decrease—fish and seafood, deer, and acorns.

## Food from the Mighty Oak

There are seven species of oak native to California, including the valley oak, black oak, live oak, and scrub oak. When fully grown, each species of oak bears anywhere from 150 to 500 pounds of acorns each year. These were ground into flour and eaten as a mush similar to grits or rice cereal. The tribes shared this bounty with grizzly bears, squirrels, birds, and insects that also depended on the nutritious nut for survival.

The acorn harvest was a joyous event held for several weeks each October, marking the beginning of the new year for the tribes. Entire villages participated in gathering the nuts with families setting up camp in individual oak groves where they held traditional "collecting rights." Boys climbed up the trees and shook limbs, while fathers poked at the ripe acorns with sticks to knock them from the branches. Women, small children, and older people picked up the bounty from the forest floor, selecting nuts without wormholes, snapping off the caps, and dropping them into large baskets placed next to the tree trunks. When the baskets were full, the acorns were emptied on an open piece of ground to dry in the sun. In this manner, a family might gather up to seventy-five pounds of acorns in one hour, or up to six hundred pounds per eight-hour day. Half this weight was shell—and an average family might consume up to three thousand pounds of acorns a year—so many long days of labor were required to procure acorns.

Harvest nights were as joyous as the days, with people visiting relatives from other villages, trading, playing games, singing, and dancing. This was also a time for teenagers to meet members of the opposite sex from distant friendly tribes—perfect candidates for marriage.

*A Paviotso fisherman uses speed and dexterity to spear salmon in a mountain lake.*

After the harvest, people returned to their villages lugging heavy baskets overflowing with acorns. The nuts were transferred to granaries—huge baskets on stilts that stood outside of each hut. To keep away insects and prevent the precious crop from becoming moldy, these granary baskets were lined with strong-smelling herbs such as mugwort.

Once safely stashed, the acorns could be eaten throughout the year. Malcolm Margolin describes the initial steps taken to prepare acorn flour:

> The preparation of acorn mush was a woman's daily occupation—almost as regular and predictable a part of

life as the rising of the sun. Each day a woman removed several handfuls of acorns from her storage baskets. She hulled them one at a time by placing them on an anvil stone, hitting them with a hammer stone, and peeling off the shells. Then she put the kernels into a stone mortar or sometimes a mortar basket (a bottomless basket glued to a rock). Sitting with the other women of the village, she pounded the acorns with a long pestle, pausing now and then to scrape the acorn flour away from the sides of the mortar with a soaproot fiber brush. Then she pounded some more. The rhythmic thumping of the women's pestles filled the air. For the Ohlones this was the sound of their village, the sound of "home."

After pounding, a woman put the flour into a shallow sifting basket which she vibrated rapidly back and forth to separate the fine flour from the coarse. Putting the fine flour

*A Native American woman prepares acorn flour for mush or fried cakes. Preparing such flour was a daily chore for the women of most California tribes.*

## Dinner from Acorns

In *The Natural World of the California Indians* Robert F. Heizer and Albert B. Elsasser describe the time-consuming steps women took in order to provide their families with food from the acorn:

"All acorns produced by the several species of California oaks contain tannin . . . (tannic acid), which is bitter in an untreated state and makes the acorns unpalatable. Two methods of removing the tannin were employed. One was to bury the whole (i.e. unshelled) acorns in mud, usually on the edge of a stream or a swamp, for a period of several months, up to a year. This mud immersion method neutralized the bitter element, so the acorns became 'sweet.' The most common method was to remove the acorn hull, grind the interior 'meat' into a flour in a stone mortar or on a flat grinding slab . . . and then pour warm water repeatedly over the flour, to leach out the tannin. A shallow concave pit was dug in the earth, lined with grass or conifer needles, and the acorn meal was put in the pit. The water was heated in a basket by dropping in hot stones that had been placed in a fire, and it was gently poured over the meal. Several such applications of warm water percolating through the meal sufficed to rid it of the bitter taste.

The leached meal was next mixed with water in a watertight basket and boiled by dropping hot stones, usually about fist size, into the gruel. The cooked mush was then edible, and was either drunk or eaten with a spoon made of half of a bivalve shell, or carved of wood or antler. . . . At times the leached acorn meal was made into a cake and baked on a flat stone heated in the fire, but most tribes preferred to consume acorns as mush. It was not customary to enhance the taste of the mush by adding spices or other flavoring."

*An Indian woman boils acorn flour to remove the bitter-tasting tannin.*

aside, she returned the coarse flour to the mortar for still more pounding.[20]

## Cuisine from the Countryside

While acorns were common to all California tribes, other food sources were determined by a tribe's location. And within these locations, a tribe might be able to utilize flora and fauna from several different ecological zones, or biozones, that yielded different types of food. For example, tribes that lived near the coast could travel to river-fed freshwater marshes where ducks, geese, and other waterfowl could be hunted. Saltwater marshes yielded shellfish such as cockles and oyster. Beaches, called strands, offered beached whales, seals, sea birds, fish, shellfish, and edible seaweed. Island tribes had little access to much of the flora and fauna found on the mainland, but people in these areas lived on seafood, fish, whale meat, sea otter, and wild cherries. For foods that they could not find at home, such as acorn meal, the island tribes bartered with their onshore relatives.

Inland, the chaparral zone was covered with shrubs that attracted deer, bear, squirrel, and other game animals. In the lower hills, grasslands were filled with rabbits and small rodents. The streamside, or riparian, woodlands of buckeye, alder, willow, grass, and herbs was home to antelope, small game, and a wide variety of birds appreciated by hunters. The mountains contained zones where tribes could gather the coveted piñon nut, sage, and larger game animals including bighorn sheep. And in the desert, tribes ate rats, snakes, rabbits, migrating birds such as geese, and plants like the prickly pear, yucca, and the mesquite pod, or screwbean. From ocean to mountain and desert, tribes moved through these zones as the year wore on, taking the best nature had to offer. Michael Baksh describes the seasonal movements of the Kumeyaay as various plants bloomed and ripened:

> [Travel] was vertical, following the ripening of major plants from canyon floor to higher mountain slopes. . . . After months of preserved vegetal food and limited game, March through May provided welcome buds, blossoms, and potherbs from canyons and lower foothills. Some people left in May for agave. . . . In early June they dried ripening cactus fruits to store in foothill caves. From June through August wild seeds ripened, and at higher altitudes wild plums and other fruits. . . . Men, women, and children worked far into the night from September to November in higher altitudes to gather and preserve acorns and sometimes piñon nuts.[21]

From these various regions, tribesmen were able to hunt young coyotes, elk, badgers, gophers, jackrabbits, wood rats, wild dogs, moles, lizards, snakes, raccoons, wildcats, foxes, songbirds, hawks, quail, doves, and other animals. The meat of these animals might be eaten raw, cooked in stews, or roasted.

Hunting techniques varied, but most animals were killed at close range by spears or arrows shot from bows. Birds were killed with a slingshot or bola—a weapon consisting of a rope with two heavy balls attached to either end. Quail were caught in noose traps, sprung by bent sticks under tension.

To catch deer in small herds, a hunter masked his human scent in an herb-filled sweat lodge, donned a mask made from a deer's head and antlers, and painted his body with camouflage patterns. Where large numbers of deer, antelope, and elk were found, tribesmen could drive the entire herd into nets, over cliffs, or into an ambush where they could be dispatched with clubs, spears, and bow and arrow.

*A Hupa elder displays a deer mask used for camouflage during the hunt.*

## The Bounty of the Sea

Along the coast, seafood was so abundant that it could simply be picked up or scooped from the water in baskets. In the winter, mussels, clams, oysters, lobsters, crabs, abalone, and other shellfish were washed up on shore by rough seas. When this happened, men, women, and children of the Chumash, Gabrielino, Luiseño, Kumeyaay, and other tribes would fan out across the beaches, picking up the creatures and tossing them into net bags.

In addition to the ocean's bounty, the silver flash of countless fish filled streams during certain times of the year. For example, the smelt run in Carmel Creek near Monterey Bay lasted twenty days. During this time, tribespeople came from near and far to scoop the fish out of the river with dip nets. The tribes were joined in their hunt by hundreds of seals and dolphins that also came to gorge on the smelt.

As the sun set, riverbanks were clouded in a haze of wood smoke as fish were gutted, cleaned, and dried over fires. This process attracted thousands of screeching gulls, pelicans, cormorants, and other seabirds hoping to feast on the scraps.

Whales were another rich source of food. Unlike tribes in the Pacific Northwest, however, the California coastal tribes did not hunt whales at sea. Instead they waited until a dead or dying whale washed up on the beach, an event that they believed to be a result of rituals and dances performed by shamans. Soon the meat was being stripped from the animal while young boys perched in the upper branches of the trees, waving sticks to keep away the ubiquitous seagulls. The meat was hung high in trees out of the reach of grizzlies; the blubber was saved in baskets and used like butter.

## Watercraft for Every Purpose

Coastal tribes did not always wait for food to come to them, however. Hunters also utilized boats—and these watercraft were as important to the tribesmen as bows and arrows. Made from tightly woven tule rushes, the canoelike watercraft could be poled or paddled in marshes, rivers, and lakes. In marshy areas, the tule canoes allowed hunters access to the thick reeds where waterfowl were abundant. Tule was also useful for making rafts, which were used as fishing platforms. And the Yokuts were in the habit of attaching several such platforms together into barges up to fifty feet long on which entire villages lived during long fishing trips.

Northern tribes such as the Yurok, Tolowa, and Wiyot made dugout canoes. These watercraft were constructed from twenty-foot-long redwood logs split in half. A passenger compartment was burned in the heartwood and laboriously smoothed to a fine finish with a stone adze. These extremely sturdy boats could be paddled on the ocean or used to navigate rushing rivers filled with rocks and boulders. Materials from old or broken boats were sometimes recycled for use in home construction.

Coastal tribes such as the Chumash also built canoes, but used wooden planks instead of tule grass. These were much more seaworthy than those of tule, and perfect for sailing out to the Santa Barbara Islands. In his 1769 account of the Gaspar de Portolá expedition, *The Discovery of San Francisco Bay*, Spanish writer Miguel Costansó describes the plank canoes and how the natives used them:

> These natives are well built and of a good disposition, very agile and alert, diligent and skillful. Their handiness and ability were at their best in the construction of their canoes, made of good pine boards, well joined and caulked, and of a pleasing form. They handle these with equal skill, and three or four men go out to

*A Yurok Indian poses in a dugout canoe constructed from a redwood log. Such vessels were strong enough to use in both the ocean and the rapids of California rivers.*

> sea in them to fish, while they will hold eight or ten men. They use long double-bladed paddles and row with indescribable agility and swiftness.[22]

In addition to fishing, such boats allowed island dwellers to bring goods to the mainland for trade, and tribesmen were often seen in their canoes transporting abalone, whale meat, fruit, and sea otter pelts to the mainland.

## The Work of Fire

Fire was another hunting tool used by the tribes, especially the Gabrielino and Chumash who set the grass on fire to drive rabbits into nets. The Yokuts also utilized fire, but for a different purpose. In the foothills of the Central Valley the tribes harvested a small, wheatlike berry from a now extinct grass. After the harvest, the Yokuts burned the fields and scattered some of the grain over the ashes, along with seeds of other desirable plants. In a few years the hillsides were covered with lush green grasses and wildflowers. Early explorers thought that these carefully created areas of vegetation were a natural occurrence and, after they forced the natives off the land, could not understand why these beautiful and beneficial plants suddenly disappeared.

Tribes also set fires to catch insects such as grasshoppers, a great delicacy that was eaten after being roasted alive in the grass fire. They also ate boiled earthworms, roasted honeybees, and smoked moth larvae. In *The Natural World of the California Indians* Robert F. Heizer and Albert B. Elsasser explain how the Monache made cricket soup:

> Gather . . . crickets early in the morning before they become too active. Dig a pit and build a fire in it, allowing it to burn down to coals. Put crickets in the pit on the coals and immediately cover with earth. From time to time extract a cricket and sample it to see if it is done. When roasted to taste, remove crickets from the pit and place in the sun to dry. The crickets can then be boiled to make soup.[23]

## The Art of Basketry

The tribes could not eat every part of the animals they caught, but they were able to use most parts of their catch for some other purpose. Tools such as needles, fishhooks, and awls were made from bone.

### Fire and Food

Desert wildfires could wipe out a Cahuilla village in a matter of minutes. But fires could also be helpful to the desert tribes, as Lowell John Bean writes in *Mukat's People: The Cahuilla Indians of Southern California:*

"On the positive side, the ashes remaining on the ground following a fire enriched the soil because of the minerals which were released. As soon as the rains came to such an area, a very rich growth of seed plants such as chia sprouted, which provided an important food for the people as well as attracting great numbers of game animals who found both food and protective covering for themselves.

Some Cahuillas have suggested that small fires were deliberately set to chase game from thick brushy areas into the open where the hunters captured them with nets and clubbed them to death. . . .

Fire was also used to protect food resources from predators. In some years immense grasshopper and locust hordes appeared which completely stripped an area of its vegetation. The Cahuilla attempted to control these predations by setting fire to the area to destroy the hordes, thus providing them with an abundant source of roasted insects of which they were very fond."

Animal parts were also important for the crafting of musical instruments. Whistles and flutes were made from bone, and deer hooves were tied in a bundle to make rattles. Rattles were also made from turtle shells filled with gravel and mounted on sticks.

While these tools were fashioned by men, the art of basket weaving was the domain of women. And these were the most finely crafted items made by the California tribes. At least seventy-eight different plants were used in basketry, including bear grass, pines, cattail, and sedges. And some plants were used in great quantities. For example, women of the Monache tribe wove baskets from the thin stalks of the deer grass flower. This was an artistic—and time-consuming—chore, with over thirty-seven hundred separate stalks needed to weave one medium-sized basket.

These handcrafted items played an important part of the daily routine throughout a person's life. Watertight baskets, woven with great skill, were used as bowls, plates, and receptacles to process and cook food. Large burden baskets transported firewood, acorns, roots, and other bulky items. Woven jars lined with a tarlike substance called asphaltum stored water. Beautiful baskets interlaced with different shells, feathers, and colored grasses displayed images of dancers, birds, rattlesnakes, bears, and geometric patterns. These were given as gifts, prized as heirlooms, and handed down for generations from mother to daughter.

## Uses for Natural Resources

While ingeniously utilizing plants for basketry, California tribes also found hundreds of other uses for the natural resources that surrounded them. Herbs and plants were used to treat headaches, cramps, wounds, and a host of other physical ailments. Alder bark tea was used to cure stomachaches, wild ginger was applied as a poultice to wounds, and yerba santa tea calmed coughs and eased sore throats. And some herbs, such as California laurel, were used as insect repellents. Boughs or leaves strewn about a house kept the huts free from fleas.

Plants and herbs were also employed in dye making. Buttercups provided yellow dye, larkspur made blue, elderberries yielded black, and mountain mahogany made red. These colors were used for decorating baskets and bows and in ceremonial face and body painting. Perhaps most startling to European explorers were the permanent plant-dyed facial tattoos worn by women.

While bark of trees yielded dye and medicine, hundreds of products were fashioned from wood, including bowls, boxes, and stools. The most common wood products were bows and arrows made from oak and other hardwoods. Arrowheads were fashioned out of obsidian, a black, glasslike stone, which was also used for making knives, scrapers, choppers, and other implements.

Some plants were favored for their toxicity. For example, dove weed and soap plant

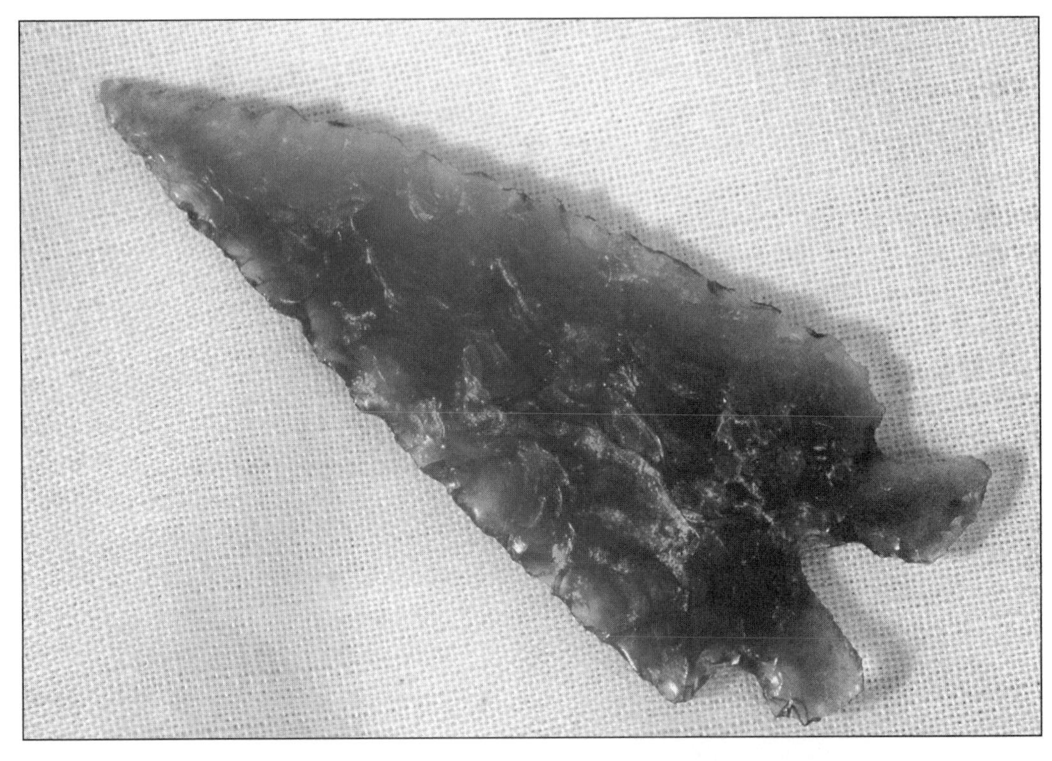

*Hunters made arrowheads like this one from obsidian by chipping small flakes until the edges were sharp. Obsidian was used to make a number of other sharp implements.*

were known to render fish unconscious. These plants were sometimes thrown in shallow pools to stupefy fish, causing them to float to the surface where they could be scooped up with baskets. Since these poisons dissipated from the fish during cooking, these foods were not harmful to humans.

Tobacco, which was smoked in clay or stone pipes, was another toxic drug used by Native Americans throughout North America. It was one of the few plants that was actively cultivated in California. Plots were cleared, the land was burned, seeds were planted, and the crop was furrowed, weeded, and harvested. Then the leaves were dried and smoked during ceremonies and rituals.

## Trade Routes

With each region containing its own specific bounty of food, the tribes traded among themselves so that the riches of the oceans, rivers, grasslands, mountains, and deserts were spread out across the state.

Native Americans in California were avid traders, and villages were connected by an extensive system of trails. Trading was not necessarily motivated by profits but for the love of exchanging goods with other tribes. In fact, tribespeople considered it rude to haggle and took whatever reasonable price was offered for an item. Of course word spread quickly in the small Indian communities, and anyone who used unfair trade practices soon developed a reputation as a miser, and others refused to barter with him. And all tribes with an abundance of a specific product were expected to share. As Malcolm Margolin writes:

> A group which lived along a rich salmon creek did not, for example, hoard its catch, but shared it with others. Visitors passing through were always given gifts of salmon, and in years of plenty the salmon-rich tribelet entertained neighbors with lavish salmon feasts. Other tribelets, in turn, reciprocated with gifts of shellfish, seeds, game, skin, nuts, or precious metals. Also, between salmon runs, or in years when the salmon catch was low, the salmon-fishing tribelet would visit its neighbors, fully expecting to be feasted and entertained.

Similarly, if a tribelet had a valuable oyster bed, mine, quarry, [tar] seep, or other resource on its territory, it would generally let other groups pass through to use it. Everyone expected this; if one tribelet tried to deny

## Clothing for a Warm Climate

The art of basketry was employed to fashion many articles of clothing, including hats, rain coats, aprons, sandals, and belts. In *California's Gabrielino Indians* Bernice Eastman Johnston describes other materials used for clothing:

"All of the early European observers of these Indians were struck with the deliberate and unabashed nudity of the men and children. The women, quite modest in contrast, wore aprons made of narrow, flexible strips of the inner bark of cottonwood or willow, hung in back, and frontflaps of many strands of twine formed from the fibers of dogbane or milkweed. Sometimes the apron at the back was of deerskin, and the men occasionally sported a small deerskin cape for the shoulders. A robe made of twisted strips of rabbit fur, woven together with milkweed or yucca-fiber twine, was useful at night [when temperatures cooled], as were deerskins. On the islands and along the coast robes made of otterskin were to be seen. Farther inland they would have been a princely possession. As a rule everyone went barefoot, although yucca-fiber sandals were used in rough country."

> others entry, war might even result. Visiting tribelets did not take entry for granted, however, but were expected to ask for proper permission and bring proper gifts.[24]

In addition to barter, California tribes paid with money in the form of strings of seashell beads. This currency originated with the Chumash of Santa Cruz Island, who were dependent on trade for many of their daily needs. This medium of exchange was described by Longinos Martínez in 1792 in a report to the Spanish government:

> In their bargaining they use . . . their *poncos* of strings of beads. This word *ponco* . . . is used for a certain measure of strings, two turns from the wrist to the extended middle finger. The value of the *ponco* depends on the esteem in which the beads are held, according to the difference in fineness and the colors that are common among them, [Spanish glass beads] being held in higher regard. . . . They make their beads out of a species of small sea snail *(caracolito)*, which they break into pieces, shaping

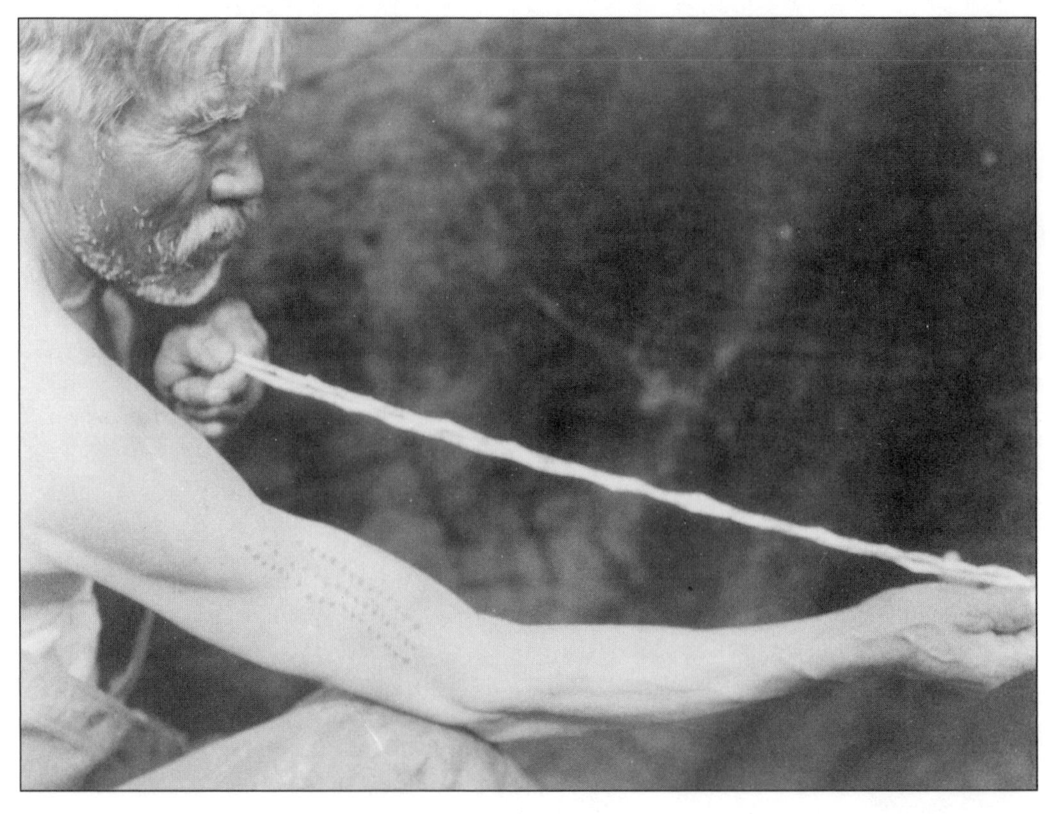

*A Chumash man measures a string of polished seashell beads to use as a form of currency.*

> them in the form of lentils, then drilling them with our needles and stringing them. After the strings have been made they rub them down until they bring them to a degree of fineness, for in their conception they have more value so. These strings of beads, and ours, are used by the men to adorn their heads. . . . They all make a show of their wealth, which they always wear in sight on their heads.[25]

This type of money was so pervasive that the sixteenth-century Spanish explorers considered eight strands of shells to be worth one silver dollar. And the beads were traded far and wide; in the 1960s a strand of shells nine thousand years old was found in a cave in Nevada, several hundred miles from the California coast.

With an active trading economy, plenty of food, a cornucopia of natural resources, and a talent for making boats, baskets, and bows, Native Americans in California lived in a manner that would have been the envy of the average European peasant. Blessed by peace and plenty, the original Californians were by any measure some of the wealthiest people anywhere in the world.

Chapter 4

# Spirits and Healing

Living in a land of pristine ocean coast, skyscraping redwoods, and astounding granite mountains, people of California felt truly blessed by the spirits. And from the fertile shores of northern California to the immaculate beaches of San Diego, California's Native Americans were deeply spiritual people who cherished their ancient religious beliefs. To these tribes the water, sun, moon, skies, winds, trees, plants, rocks, and animals were all alive with gods and goddesses. These deities were able to bestow blessings—or wreak havoc—depending on dozens of signs and omens.

Native Americans paid homage to their deities in dozens of ritual feasts and dances. These were held at regular intervals throughout the year and were marked by chanted prayers, rhythmic drumming, elaborate costumes, frenzied dancing, and feasting.

Religious rites were also held during milestones in an individual's life: the naming of a baby, the attainment of puberty, marriage, and death. Other rituals and rites were performed in the event of misfortunes such as sickness, drought, famine, and war.

Behind the rituals, tribespeople held a deep respect for nature, for it was within nature that their gods and goddesses existed. In this way, their religious beliefs inspired them to be custodians of nature and protectors of the environment. And the holiest and most blessed of all beings were human families, who were valued above all else.

## Families and Clans

Many California tribes were divided into two basic familylike units, called moieties. These groups took their names from animals believed to have great spiritual powers—and there were smaller units, called clans, that sometimes used the same animals. For example the Gabrielino, Serrano, and Cahuilla all divided their moieties into two clans—the Coyote and Wildcat. These names were not chosen at random but have deep religious significance for the tribes. Wildcat people worshiped the lynx because the animal possessed such admirable qualities as stealth, fearlessness, and acute senses. People of other clans were spiritually tied to the mythical creature named Coyote, an animal with supernatural powers who was credited with having helped create the world. Coyote was also a "trickster" who has caused all sorts of mischief, as Malcolm Margolin explains in *The Way We Lived:*

> The trickster . . . is at the same time good and evil, crafty and foolish, godlike and scroungy. He is both the prankster and the dupe. . . . [The] trickster generally took his name from the [coyote, a] sly dog-like animal who skulked around the outskirts of villages, hunting gophers, scavenging the refuse piles, and occasionally stealing salmon and deer meat from the drying racks.
>
> In a typical Coyote story the "hero" sets off on a foolish mission and gets into trouble, as he falls victim to his own irrepressible curiosity and compulsions.[26]

Because Coyote's actions were a mixture of good and bad, embracing the best and

*A group of modern Native American dancers lines up to participate in a religious rite.*

worst parts of human nature, the tribes believed that Coyote was similar in his actions to people. And tribes such as the Cahuilla believed that Coyote, along with the Wildcat, were related to the twin creators of the world, Tamaioit and Mukat respectively.

While moieties are based on supernatural legends, they serve several practical purposes. In addition to serving as channels of kinship for large numbers of widely scattered tribes, they also determined marriage customs. For example, tribes were strictly forbidden from marrying members of their own moiety. That is, a Coyote could only marry a Wildcat and vice versa. This custom helped to prevent the passing on to children of inherited disorders that can result when close relatives marry.

## A Clan's Sacred Bundle

Cahuilla that lived around Palm Springs were divided into three clans: the "day-

### Coyote and Falcon Create the World

Among the tribes of central and northern California, Coyote is a prominent figure in dozens of tales and is believed to be the cocreator of the world. This legend from *The Way We Lived*, edited by Malcolm Margolin, is one of many that tell how Coyote created the world:

"Falcon proposed that Coyote create human beings. Coyote replied that it would mean a great deal of work, but Falcon insisted that it be done. . . . Accordingly Coyote went out and threw himself upon the ground, simulating a dead body. Presently a large flock of crows and buzzards gathered about and commenced to peck at Coyote's rump. He kept perfectly still until the birds had eaten a large hole in one side and were within. He then caused the hole to close very suddenly and caught a considerable number of them. He took them home and Falcon plucked them. 'Now,' said Coyote, 'we will go out in the country and put these feathers in every direction.' On each hill they placed one buzzard and one crow feather. The crow feathers became the common people and the buzzard feathers, the chiefs. As Coyote deposited the feathers he named each place, and on the following day there were people living in all these localities.

Coyote then said to Falcon, 'Now that there is a new people, we shall have to become animals. I shall be coyote; no one will miss me. You shall be falcon, and everyone shall know you as chief.' Straightway all of the then-existing animal people were transmuted and became birds and mammals as Coyote directed."

break people," the "good people," and the "rock people." The first two were Wildcats and the last was Coyote. Each clan had its own ceremonial head, known as a *net*, who lived in a ceremonial dance house.

*Nets* were the keepers of the sacred bundle, large interwoven bunches of reeds that were up to three feet wide and twenty feet long. Such sacred bundles were central to every tribe's religious ceremonies and contained symbols of great power such as collections of eagle feathers and pelvic bones of grizzly bears.

Sacred bundles belonged to the entire clan and were kept in a special room within the dance house. Keeping the bundle safe was an important responsibility for the *net,* who also determined the timing of rituals and the collection of food for use during feasts. *Nets* also acted as judges when disputes erupted between neighbors. In addition, he decided the best times to perform tasks, such as harvesting acorns, and was responsible for picking campsites where villagers would stay.

## Shamans and Powerful Medicine

One of the most important men within each moiety was the shaman. The tribes sometimes referred to shamans as "medicine men" or "witch men," even though some shamans were women.

Shamans were believed to hold supernatural powers passed down from the gods and goddesses who had created the world. To achieve this position required a lifetime of training, and the duties of the shaman were extremely difficult. He was called upon by tribe members to consult with the deities and was expected to convey the desires of the gods to the people. He was also asked to relieve physical and spiritual pain, preside over religious ceremonies, and teach young men the ways of the shaman.

As a reward for his work, the shaman was provided for by his people who supplied him with food, shelter, clothing, firewood, and other necessities. But he was obligated, in return, to continually perform magic rituals that would bless his tribe with a steady supply of food. He was also expected to cast spells to control the weather, for everyone wanted to see the rains come, but not so heavily as to cause flooding and other problems. And since tribespeople believed that disease was caused by witches or the spirits of animals that have been mistreated, shamans had to perform rituals to appease these spirits and prevent illness. If someone was sick, shamans would treat the affliction by performing acts aimed at banishing the evil spirits that were held responsible.

Often a shaman would blow tobacco smoke over a patient's body or attempt to access the evil spirit by sucking it out of the person's mouth, either through a stone tube or directly with the lips. After the sucking ritual, the shaman might remove a pebble, feather, or other object kept in his mouth that represented the illness-causing spirit.

Shamans used special tools such as quartz crystals and soapstone carvings of whales, bears, coyotes, deer, and other animals that were imbued with magic powers.

## The Bear Cult

While some shamans tended to the general religious needs of the people, many tribes developed cults dedicated to various animals such as deer and bear. For example, in *Breath of the Sun*, Chumash tribesman Fernando Librado writes of Bear medicine men who lived in caves and dressed in bearskins stuffed with grass to give them a natural shape. It was believed that the abilities of these bear-men were anything but natural, however. A tribesman told Librado

> that inside the bear suit were three cords, each with a loop for a finger. The cords were operated by three fingers on the left hand: the index finger was for walking, the middle finger was for running, and the ring finger was for turning. The index and middle fingers joined together would cause the bear to go swiftly. . . . The right hand was left free for giving blows. If you didn't know the combination, you were likely to make it go swiftly and bump up against the side of a tree or mountain or something. These forces were supernatural, and I think the Indians used herbs in this regard. A man would of course do his part [that is, walking, running, or turning], but otherwise he would not be able to put on the speed that he could when he was assisted by these supernatural forces. The thing must have had many superstitions.[27]

*A female shaman of the Hupa tribe poses with her healing implements and jewelry.*

## The Cult of Chungichnish

While many tribes believed that Coyote created the world, the most popular cult in Southern California was dedicated to Chungichnish, who was said to have created the world by sending a man representing the sky to join with a woman from Earth. Together this couple made animals as well as sand, rocks, trees, shrubs, herbs and grasses, and finally its people. After the world was created, Chungichnish sent

## Cosmic Rock Art

Some of the rock art created by shamans hundreds of years ago may still be viewed in remote locations in Southern California. The website maintained by the federal Bureau of Land Management (BLM) provides details about this art:

"Pictographs are rock paintings, made from mineral earths like red ocher mixed with oil, and applied to rock surfaces with the fingers or an animal tail brush. . . .

Petroglyphs are rock engravings, made by using a fist-sized stone cobble to hammer or peck a design into a rock surface. . . .

In many areas of the state, shamans or medicine men made rock art to preserve a record of their visionary trances. Shamans used fasting and native tobacco to enter a trance during ritual vision quests. These were believed visits to the supernatural, where the shaman obtained supernatural power, often in the form of animal spirit helpers. Shamans also sought visions to cure, make rain, find lost objects or bewitch an enemy.

Many pictographs and petroglyphs appear to be geometric designs. These were visionary images that served as 'signs of supernatural power.' Archaeologists call these geometric images entoptics ('behind the eye') because they represent light patterns that are generated by our nervous system during a trance. Animal figures were animal spirit helpers; human designs were images of the shaman or other human-like spirits seen in the vision. Because the shaman was believed able to change into his spirit helper while in the supernatural, some motifs show a human transforming into a spirit animal."

*A shaman makes a rock painting of a vision by chiseling a design into the surface.*

observers, such as Raven, to watch over the people. Through his observers, Chungichnish acted as the lawgiver who sat in judgment of wrongdoers and punished them with spiders, nettles, and rattlesnakes.

The Chungichnish cult is found among many Southern California tribes including the Luiseño, Chumash, Kumeyaay, and others but is thought to have originated among the Gabrielino living on Santa Catalina Island. Members of the cult built ceremonial structures from brush but open to the sky. Medicine bundles made from coyote pelts and stuffed with arrows, feathers, animal horns, claws, and condor beaks were placed inside the huts. Members of the Chungichnish cult wore ceremonial skirts and headpieces constructed from hundreds of eagle and condor feathers. The rest of the body was painted red, black, and white.

*Jimsonweed (pictured) was made into a powerful hallucinogenic drug that many tribes used in initiation ceremonies.*

Only men were allowed in the Chungichnish cult, and they were initiated at an important ceremony that took place when boys were adolescents of about sixteen. At that time, the young men took a powerful hallucinogenic drug called *toloache* made from jimsonweed *(Datura stramonium)*. While under the drug's influence, the teens experienced wild hallucinations and, at the same time, were subjected to long sermons by cult shamans.

To prepare for their *toloache* ceremony, the initiates fasted for about three days. They were then painted black and red, dressed in an elaborate headdress and skirt made from feathers, and instructed to make a ground sand painting that contained cosmic figures such as the Milky Way, animal spirits, and so on.

After taking the jimsonweed potion, wild dancing ensued until the young men fell into a narcotic stupor. Each initiate was carried to a quiet place where he would experience vivid dreams, or visions, sometimes of an animal, such as a coyote, bear, crow, rattlesnake, or raven. If this happened, the animal would become the young man's guardian spirit and protect and counsel him throughout his life.

Among the Luiseño tribe, the ingestion of the drug was followed by punishing tests of endurance. Some of these torments were described by Bernice Eastman Johnston in *California's Gabrielino Indians:*

> [Young] men were tested and hardened by methods that seem quite extreme. They were whipped with nettles and stung by myriads of red ants, sometimes while lying in a disturbed nest of those aggressive insects. Music from a deerbone flute and dancing by the men added a festive note to the observance. The conclusion of this period was attested by a branding, usually on the upper right arm. A patch of dry, highly combustible leaves of the California mugwort was set on fire, raising a large blister. A scar resulted and any male who went through life without this sign was considered to be a weakling and utterly unfit.[28]

Jimsonweed was used by other tribes such as the Monache, Cahuilla, and Yokuts, in less intense circumstances and with no connection with Chungichnish. These tribes gave the potion to young men and women between the ages of sixteen and twenty, in the belief that it would help them gain long life, health, and contact with a spiritual helper. Although none were compelled to take it, for most teens this was a once-in-a-lifetime experience, and some who wanted to become shamans took it repeatedly.

## Initiating Girls into Adulthood

Upon experiencing their first menstruation, young women of the Luiseño tribe were also subjected to tough initiations. In one ceremony a girl was expected to fast for three days while lying utterly still, buried under grass and sand with an open-weave basket over her face in a superheated underground sweat lodge. She was allowed to leave only once every twenty-four hours when the hot sauna rocks were replenished. Bernice Eastman Johnston describes the customs that followed the pit initiation:

> A ground-painting was made for the girl's ceremony. . . . For them, as for the boys, moral lectures were given, telling them how to conduct themselves in order to be popular socially and avoid the calamities that awaited anyone who annoyed the ever-watchful Chungichnish. A girl must be industrious and never a gadabout; she must remember to bathe daily, to be hospitable, and have a straightforward manner without deceit.[29]

Girls were also closely questioned about their dreams during this initiation ceremony so that they might find their guiding spirits. Then the young woman's face was painted, she was given anklets and bracelets woven of shell and human hair, and a feast was held in her honor.

In tribes such as the Ohlone, in the months after the ceremony, the woman received her first facial tattoos. This was done by an older woman who etched designs in the teen's face, breasts, and shoulders with a very sharp stone before applying charcoal dust and colored plant juice into the wounds. When healed, the black, blue, and green designs provided intimate information to all who looked at them. Some tattoos held magical significance, but others told of the girl's clan and genealogical lineage. In this way, a young man who wanted to marry the girl would instantly know if she was of a compatible clan, or of the same clan and therefore not marriageable. Malcolm Margolin describes the importance of these tattoos:

> For a grown woman to be without such tattoos would have been shameful and lewd, an act of indecent exposure. . . . In this way a girl bore for the rest of her life the marks of her tribelet and lineage. Yet, in a less literal way, this was the fate of every Ohlone . . . [who] would bear the stamp of his or her culture. In these closed, almost unchanging societies, the individualist had no place. It was not the role of the younger generation to be different or step out of line. Their only role was to follow the correct way.[30]

## Marriage Rites and Rituals

After the rituals initiating adolescents into adulthood, young men and women began to think of marriage. Men were considered to be of marriageable age at about eighteen when they were good enough hunters and homebuilders to provide for a family. Women married younger, at about fifteen, when they were able to cook, gather plants, weave baskets, and perform the other tasks carried out by their mothers. Unmarried pregnancy was considered a disgrace and young women tried to remain virgins until they were married. Most men were married to one woman, but powerful sachems, warriors, or other tribal leaders might have more than one wife.

Most tribes shared the practice of arranged marriages. In *Aboriginal Society in Southern California* William Duncan Strong describes the marriage customs of the Mountain Cahuilla:

> Childhood betrothals arranged between parents were common, in which case frequent presents to the family of the girl were paid by that of the boy. . . . The boy's mother would take presents of venison, acorn meal, or perhaps baskets to the girl's family and make her request. If the girl's parents were agreeable the presents were accepted, and the girl might return with her mother-in-law. . . . The net of the boy's clan then invited all the clan members and all relatives of both the boy and girl to a feast in the dance house. . . . The girl was instructed in her new duties by her mother-in-law, and the newly married pair lived with the boy's parents. If they did not get along well together the girl might gather up all her personal possessions and return to her own house, in which case there was no return of presents. No stigma was attached to her and she might marry again at any time. Should a wife be faithless the husband could send her

home. There seems to have been no feeling that a husband should fight or kill a wife's lover; he merely let the wife go if he could not or did not care to keep her.[31]

## Babies and Children

Marriage led to children, and there were many traditions surrounding childbirth. After a baby was born, older female relatives conducted ceremonies with the mother and child that could last up to a week. The baby's father and his family provided herbs, food, and other items for the mother and child who moved into a pit warmed with hot stones. Herbs with religious and medicinal purposes were placed in the pit, and the mother drank herbal potions. She was forbidden to eat salt and meat, however. Friends and family gathered around at the ceremonial hut and offered useful gifts, in the manner of a baby shower. The family, in turn, provided a luxurious feast for the guests.

In most tribes, children went unnamed or were simply given often humorous nicknames such as "Grasshopper." At age six to nine, children were given formal names at an important ceremony performed before the entire village. The parents often asked a respected tribal elder to bestow a name upon the child that would also bring the blessings of the spirits. These names sometimes came to the elder in a dream; in other cases a deceased relative was remembered. And the child might be given two names, one secret and one to be used in public. This prevented an enemy from using the person's real name for evil purposes.

*A Hupa child sits comfortably bundled in a woven carrier designed to be set aside while the mother works.*

## An Eighteenth-Century Death Ceremony

In 1775 Spanish explorer Lieutenant Pedro Fages used European cultural terms to describe a mourning ceremony he witnessed among the Chumash. This translation of his account is reprinted in *California*, vol. 8 of *The Handbook of North American Indians*:

"When any Indian dies, they carry the body to the . . . place near the village dedicated to their idols. There they celebrate the mortuary ceremony, and watch all the following night, some of them gathered about a huge fire until daybreak; then come all the rest (men and women) and four of them begin the ceremony in this wise. One Indian smoking tobacco in a large stone pipe, goes first; he is followed by the other three, all passing thrice around the body; but each time he passes the head, his companions lift the animal skin with which it is covered, that the priest may blow upon it three mouthfuls of smoke. On arriving at the feet, they all four together stop to sing I know not what manner of laudation. Then come the near and remote relatives of the deceased, each one giving the chief celebrant a string of beads, something over a [hand] span in length. Then immediately there is raised a sorrowful outcry and lamentation by all the mourners. When this sort of solemn response is ended, the four ministers take up the body, and all the Indians follow them singing to the cemetery."

## Honoring the Dead

Just as ceremonies and rituals welcomed a child into the world, elaborate rites were held at the end of life. When a Cahuilla died, the body was cremated along with his or her worldly possessions. It was believed that the dead person could use these items in the afterlife. The Yokuts buried their dead in the area where their childhood home stood. The Ohlone deposited the bodies of their important warriors and chiefs into the huge shellmounds that were left from seafood harvests. While some anthropologists believed that these mounds were simply dumps for food scraps, this notion is challenged on *The Muwekma Ohlone* website:

> These final resting-places are in fact, formal cemeteries and mortuary mounds of earth with areas that were also used for cremation. Many of these mortuary mounds contain some shell, ash, bone and charcoal, but evidence suggests that these were by-products of funerals, annual "Cry" or mourning ceremonies, cremation-

> related activities, [left by] many people attending the funerals and other related ceremonies for over a period of several days.[32]

## Powerful Magic

The ceremonies of life's great changes were among the dozens of religious rituals, ceremonies, and festivals held by the California tribes throughout the year. In fact, there was hardly any activity in which the blessing of the deities was not invoked. Women blessed the beautiful baskets they wove, while men honored the gods for luck during the hunt by painting their bows, arrows, and spears with symbols of the revered supernatural beings. Acorn harvests proceeded with ritual and ceremony, as did fishing and trading trips.

All ceremony, ritual, and religion was accompanied by dance and song, and nearly every tribal activity had its music and dance associated with mythical creatures and legends. Tribes such as the Ohlone built a variety of instruments, including whistles, rattles, and drums, to back the songs. These were all cleverly constructed from natural materials. For example, whistles were made from thin hollow bird bones, flutes were carved from alder wood, and effective rattles were made by attaching dried butterfly cocoons to wooden handles.

From the birth of a baby to the death of a tribal elder, the spiritual dedication of the Native American was as natural as breathing. And the powerful magic of the tribes of California has been credited with their success and survival over past millennia.

## Chapter 5

# Clash of Cultures

With plenty of resources, low population numbers, well-established trade practices, and far-flung territories separated by formidable natural barriers, the tribes of California were relatively peaceful to one another. But, as with any other human population, conflicts arose, and some were dealt with violently.

Warfare among the tribes was usually caused by one group seeking revenge on another rather than for material gain or territorial conquest. This might have been retribution for theft, or murder, or even from the belief that someone from another tribe had cast an evil spell on an individual. And if tribes did clash, grudges were often carried for long periods of time, even generations. But unlike tribes in the plains and along the East Coast, California tribes did not have warrior societies where combat was practiced and planned for almost constantly.

When clashes did ensue, the primary weapons were bows and arrows, rocks, and occasionally spears. Some tribes used hardwood war clubs with bulbous heads on handles up to three feet long. Before combat, warriors painted their faces and decorated their bodies with feathers.

Battles were most often carried out as surprise ambushes with twenty or thirty warriors jumping down at the victims from behind rocks or trees. Other times, warriors might attack a village before dawn, using clubs and bows and arrows to disable unsuspecting sleepers. Captives were killed on the spot, often by decapitation. Sometimes, as a prelude to death, captives were tortured in front of the entire village.

Often, hostilities only went as far as name calling, as Heizer writes about the Gabrielino in *California:*

> More common than warfare, and involving considerably less people, were feuds that passed from father to son, often for many generations. Hostilities were vented through ritualized "song fights," some lasting as long as eight days. Songs, obscene

and insulting in nature and sung in the vilest language possible, were accompanied by stomping and trampling the ground, symbolizing the subjugation of the opponent.[33]

## Missions and Slavery

With little more than bows and arrows, the California tribes were singularly unprepared for the arrival of European soldiers fully armed with cannons, muskets, pistols, knives, and swords. The first of these expeditions was led by Juan Rodriguez Cabrillo, a Portuguese explorer employed by Spain. The explorers visited the San Diego area briefly in 1542 and engaged in a skirmish with Kumeyaay warriors who rained arrows down on their camp, wounding three men. Cabrillo quickly left, sailing north along the coast,

### The Gabrielino at War

Although the California tribes were not as warlike as some to the east, hostilities could be long lasting and deadly, as Heizer explains in *California:*

"Although nineteenth-century writers often characterized the Gabrielino as timid and peaceful, the earlier chroniclers paint a different picture. A state of constant enmity existed between some coastal and prairie-mountain groups . . . [and] intervillage conflicts among the Gabrielino were so frequent and of such intensity that inland Gabrielino were effectively prevented by coastal Gabrielino from reaching the sea for fishing and trading purposes. This concern with war as more than a defensive or rare occurrence is further supported by the occurrence of reed armor, war clubs, swords, and large and heavy bows used for warfare, as well as the hunting of big game. While these 'wars' were not lengthy, they were deadly and often involved several villages.

Armed conflict could arise for a number of reasons: failure of a chief to return a gift during a ceremony, . . . abduction of women, trespassing, or sorcery (it was generally assumed that neighboring groups were using supernatural powers for harm). In the event of a potential conflict, a war council was called by an official crier (smoke signals were also used to call people from distant villages) with all potentially involved villages attending, and the pros and cons of going to war were discussed. A decision to go to war was not lightly made, since warfare involved not only the warriors, but also old men, women, and even children . . . the last two groups carrying the food and supplies."

mapping the shoreline, and visiting Santa Catalina Island, Monterey Bay, and Point Reyes near San Francisco.

Although a few other European explorers passed through the region over the next several centuries, it was not until the 1760s that the visitors had a profound and destructive impact on the native tribes. At that time Russian fur traders were commonly found hunting seal and sea otter in Northern California. Spain wanted to prevent Russia from claiming the area, so the Spanish king Carlos sent Governor Gaspar de Portolá, Junípero Serra, a Catholic priest of the Franciscan order, and several hundred soldiers from Mexico to settle Alta California. They arrived and founded San Diego in July 1769.

*A statue glorifies Juan Rodriguez Cabrillo, a Portuguese explorer employed by Spain who discovered San Diego.*

The goals of the Spanish were twofold: to convert the Native Americans to Christianity and to extend the Spanish domain over North America. But common sense suggested that the Spanish would be well advised to accomplish their task peacefully. Daniel Fogel elaborates in *Junípero Serra, the Vatican, and Enslavement Theology:*

> Peaceful conquest of the Indians was the Spanish watchword in California. The vast territory had to be secured for the Spanish empire, yet precious few Spanish and Mexican colonists were available to settle the land. Moreover, the Pacific coast of Califor-

## The Friendly Chumash

Eighteenth-century Spanish found the Chumash to be extremely hospitable, generous, and friendly—sometimes too friendly—as Miguel Costansó writes in *The Discovery of San Francisco Bay:*

"The natives of this village immediately came to [our] camp . . . bringing fish, roasted or grilled in barbecue, for us to eat while their canoes, then out fishing, were returning with fresh fish. These canoes landed on the beach shortly afterwards, and brought an abundance of bonito and bass, which they gave us and offered in such quantity that we might have loaded the pack animals with fish if we had had the facilities to salt and prepare it. Moreover, they gave us fish dried without salt (this they do not use in their victuals) which we took as a precaution, and it was of great service to us on the journey. . . .

The natives, not content with making us presents of their eatables, wished, furthermore, to give us a feast . . . in order to merit our approval and praise. In the afternoon the leaders . . . of each town came, one after the other, adorned according to their custom—painted and decked with feathers. . . .

[Their] dancing continued all the afternoon, and we had hard work to rid ourselves of them. Finally we sent them away, earnestly recommending them, by means of signs, not to come back during the night to disturb us; but in vain. At nightfall they returned with a large retinue of clowns or jugglers, playing whistles, the noise of which grated upon the ears. It was to be feared that they would stampede our horses, and, for this reason, the commander, with his officers and some soldiers, went out to receive them. These gave the natives some glass beads, and intimated to them that if they came back to disturb our sleep, they would no longer be our friends and we would give them a bad reception. This was a sufficient measure to cause them to retire and to leave us in peace for the remainder of the night."

nia was already densely populated with native peoples. The Indians themselves had to become the main population base for Spanish rule over California.[34]

In order to accomplish this goal, between 1769 and 1823 Franciscans built a continuous chain of twenty-one missions that stretched from San Diego to Sonoma, north of San Francisco. Each mission was about a day's journey on horseback from the next, along a coastal path called El Camino Real, or the King's Road. The Spanish also set up a presidio, or military post, next to each mission. Soldiers at the presidios were used by the friars to keep order among the tribes now referred to as Mission Indians.

In the beginning, to lure the Native Americans into the mission system, the friars showered them with cheap gifts such as colored cloth, glass beads, and metal trinkets. Relations were so good that Native Americans, glad to help their new neighbors, worked to build the first missions, which at the time were modest adobe structures. But while the tribespeople looked at this sharing as a cultural exchange, the Europeans had other motives. In *"We Are Not Savages"* Joel R. Hyer presents this indictment of the goals of the Spaniards and the means by which they achieved them:

*This bell tower stands near the site of the Mission San Diego de Alcala, the first of twenty-one missions built in California.*

> Spanish missionaries intended not only to Christianize California's First Peoples, but also to alter their lifestyles and obliterate their cultures. After either luring Indians into the missions with food and European goods or forcing them into these institutions with the assistance of soldiers, padres attempted to teach them basic Catholic beliefs and baptize them. . . . Once missionaries baptized Indians, they refused to allow them to leave the missions. Hoping to mold them into a docile labor force, friars instructed native peoples in various trades, such as masonry and carpentry. They sought to destroy native languages by teaching Indians only in Spanish and by punishing those who spoke in their native tongue. Regarding indigenous cultures as worthless, priests attempted to halt native puberty rites . . . , and

other rituals while introducing Indian peoples to baptism and Mass. They also strived to replace native oral traditions, such as the accounts of . . . Coyote . . . with stories from the Bible.[35]

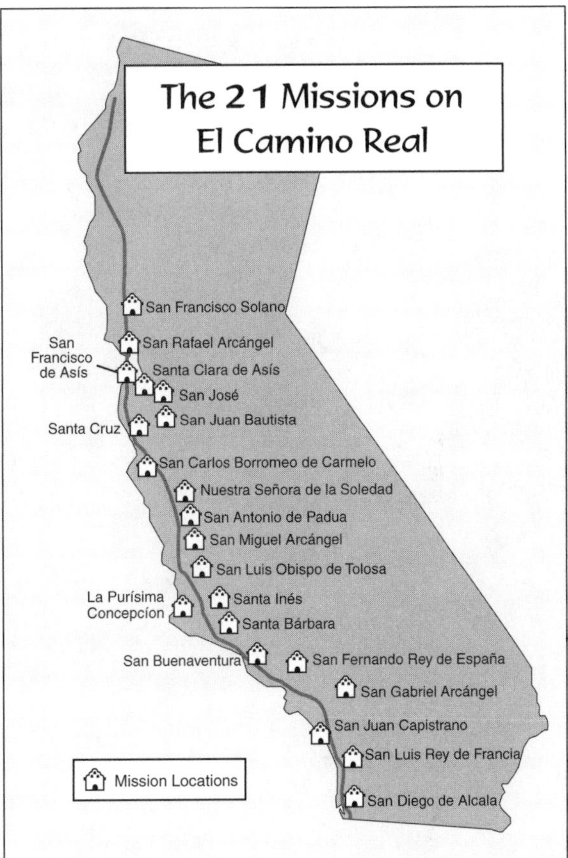


## Destruction of the People

The mission system did more than destroy Native American culture. It instituted a system of slavery similar to what African Americans were experiencing in the American South and elsewhere. And this system resulted in near total extinction of California Native Americans. Today such widespread annihilation of a populace is identified as genocide.

The Franciscan friars employed a policy called *congregación*, or concentration, where baptized Native Americans were herded into one location where they could be used as a free source of labor. In traditional native villages, the population might contain one to three hundred people. But as the Spanish forced the tribes into the villages, called pueblos, around the missions, there might be one thousand natives from several different tribes crowded into small, dirty adobe dormitories with extremely unsanitary living conditions.

For the people who traditionally knew little of bad health, sickness became all too common. The Europeans had inadvertently brought a host of deadly diseases to the Americas to which the native tribes had no immunity. Almost immediately, Native Americans began dying of measles, cholera, smallpox, scarlet fever, diphtheria, yellow fever, typhoid fever, meningitis, whooping cough, syphilis, influenza, and dysentery.

A small sample of the grim statistics recorded in official documents demonstrates the path of destruction caused by these diseases: Shortly after the founding of the Santa Clara mission in 1777, a respiratory disease killed the majority of Ohlone in the region. In January 1806 a measles outbreak

*Mission Indians of Southern California make baskets and spin hair to make rope. Indians attached to the missions faced a harsh existence centered around manual labor.*

that had started in San Diego quickly spread up the coast, reaching San Francisco within three months. This killed sixteen hundred Native Americans, including all children under age ten in some places. At the Santa Clara mission alone, 88 women, 64 men, 36 girls, and 38 boys died from the measles contagion. In that year, the total native child mortality rate was over 33 percent, and in the sixty years that the mission system was in place, a full 50 percent of Native American children died before the age of five. As a result of such losses, the Native American population of California plunged from a high of three hundred thousand in 1769 to around one hundred thousand in 1849.

## A Brutal Way of Life

For the tribes who were forced to live on the missions, epidemics were only part of the misery. Because they did not speak Spanish, few tribespeople understood that, once baptized, they had entered a class known as neophytes and were considered permanent vassals of the Catholic Church.

Mission Indians were forced to work from sunup to sundown. Men herded livestock, plowed fields, and made adobe bricks from straw and mud. Women cooked, made candles, and spun fabric from wool and made it into clothing. Age did not excuse one from working. Children and old people carried sand and straw for the brick makers, stoked fires, and made soap. This was the schedule six days a week with Mass before and after work. Sundays were reserved for six hours of worship.

Order was kept by soldiers, and those Native Americans who did not go along with the program were treated brutally. Men and women were forced to work with ankles clad in iron chains. Whippings with leather ropes, lariats, and canes were common for such offenses as stealing food in the face of starvation. For offenses such as running away to escape the slavery, neophytes might receive twenty-five lashes. The penalty for attacking a friar was twenty-five lashes for nine consecutive days, and a whipping every Sunday for nine Sundays.

## Harsh Treatment at the Missions

On occasion, some Native Americans attempted to escape the harsh conditions they found at the missions. In 1797 a group ran away from the Mission Dolores in San Francisco, but were quickly caught. Upon their return each person was asked why he ran away. The following are among the reasons recorded by the mission and published in *The Other Californians* by Robert F. Heizer and Alan F. Almquist.

"He had been flogged for leaving without permission. . . . Also, he ran away because he was hungry."

"He was frightened at seeing how his friends were always being flogged."

"When he wept over the death of his wife and children, he was ordered whipped five times by Father Antonio Danti."

"His mother, two brothers, and three nephews died, all of hunger, and he ran away so that he would not also die."

"His wife sinned with a rancher, and the priest beat him for not taking care of her."

"They made him work all day without giving him or his family anything to eat. Then, when he went out one day to find food, Father Danti flogged him."

"After going one day to the presidio to find food, when he returned Father Danti refused him his ration, saying to go to the hills and eat hay."

"When his son was sick, they would give the boy no food, and he died of hunger."

"Twice when he went out to hunt food or to fish, Father Danti had him whipped."

## The End of the Mission System

In 1821 Mexico achieved independence from Spain, and California and its missions became part of Mexico. The new government gave all Native Americans citizenship and, although it did not give them ownership, allowed them right of occupation on tribal lands. The status of the coastal tribes changed little, however. Soldiers, now Mexican, continued to force Native Americans to work for friars who retained control of the missions.

In 1833 the Mexican Congress decided it was time to reduce the power of the missions and ordered them secularized, that is, taken away from the church and turned over to nonreligious owners. The decree stated that the Native Americans were entitled to half the mission property as well as half the tools, livestock, and seeds stored at the missions.

This was not as beneficial to the tribes as it might have been. Confusion followed as the neophytes, weary from years of abuse, ran away from the missions. Few understood that they were entitled to valuable holdings that they had created with their own toil. Instead, a huge landgrab followed, as powerful friars, military officers, and cattle ranchers seized the best lands along with three-quarters of a million cows, pigs, sheep, and other livestock. By 1846, 8 million acres of mission land was broken up into eight hundred large, privately owned cattle ranches, called ranchos.

Owners of ranchos heartlessly oppressed the Native Americans, forcing them into near slavery, paying them only in alcohol, which ruined many lives and contributed to the destruction of the people. Daniel Fogel describes how this affected most California natives:

> The new aristocrats relocated entire Indian villages onto their estates to employ the Indians as full time laborers; where they needed only part time labor, they let the Indians continue living in their home villages, conscripting them for the harvests and other seasonal tasks. The Indian laborers . . . were subject to physical punishment for even petty violations of the work rules.[36]

Some tribespeople successfully fled the mission system, moving to the growing pueblos of Los Angeles, San Diego, and San Jose, where they practiced trades such as horse shoeing, candle making, and cabinetmaking that they had learned at the missions. Others, facing starvation, were forced into lives of dire poverty that included petty thievery, begging, gambling, and prostitution. The luckiest among the neophytes were taken in by northern and inland tribelets that had maintained their independence, those called "wild Indians" by the Mexicans.

## An Extremely High Toll

Although the era of "missionization" had finally ground to a halt, an extremely high toll was paid by Native Americans of Cali-

*A gravestone in a Northern California churchyard commemorates the members of the Ohlone tribe who lost their lives to European disease.*

fornia. Of the 53,600 natives who were baptized by mission priests between 1769 and 1845, only 15,000 survived. Meanwhile, disease had killed nearly two-thirds of all tribespeople. Within one generation, the ten-thousand-year collective history of California's native population had been reduced to the sadness of a few survivors. Their despair is encompassed in the voice of one unnamed neophyte from the Mission Dolores: "I am very old . . . my people were once around me like the sands of the shore . . . many . . . many. They have all passed away. They have died like the grass . . . they have gone to the mountains. . . . I had a son. I loved him. When the palefaces came he went away. I do not know where he is. I am a Christian Indian. I am all that is left of my people. I am alone."[37]

## The Calm Before the Storm

The Native Americans of California suffered greatly under Spanish and Mexican rule, but for some who lived away from the missions, life had changed little. In the north, tribes such as the Pomo, Miwok, Yuki, and Yurok traded peacefully with Russian and American fur buyers. While they were exposed to several devastating epidemics, their cultures remained largely intact.

In the central and southern parts of the state, the Kumeyaay, Cahuilla, Monache, and some Yokuts continued to practice their ancient ways, supplemented by guns, horses, and farming practices taken from their association with the Europeans and Mexicans. As Daniel Fogel writes, most "of their cultures and languages survived, and they still formed a large majority of the California population. They seemed to have a fighting chance to reassert their cultures and regain their numbers."[38] But whatever hope could be found among the inland tribes was about to be destroyed.

By the 1840s there were hundreds of Americans living in California, and in June 1846 a ragtag army of Americans captured the presidio at Sonoma and proclaimed freedom from Mexican rule. On July 7, 1846, Commodore John D. Sloat, commander of the U.S. naval forces along the California coast, ordered the United States flag raised at Monterey and claimed California for the United States. After a brief war, the Mexicans were forced to surrender a large portion of territory to the United States, including present-day New Mexico, Arizona, and California. On February 2, 1848, the two countries signed the Treaty of Guadalupe Hidalgo, ending the Mexican War and ceding California to the United States.

On January 24, just nine days before the treaty was signed, a Miwok laborer named Jim was building a grain mill on a ranch in the Sierra foothills owned by Johann Sutter. Jim found a nugget of gold in the American River and handed it to a carpenter named James Wilson Marshall who took credit for the discovery.

## Americans Rush In

News of gold in California quickly spread all over the United States, Mexico, South America, and even to Europe, Australia, and China. Within months, fortune-seekers were flooding into the region from all over the world. Whereas the population of the state had been a few thousand in 1848, in 1849 alone about seventy-five thousand miners, called forty-niners, came to California. Almost all of the forty-niners were men, and many of them were dishonest characters out to get rich quick. These people cared little about Native American land rights, much less their culture and society. As Daniel Fogel writes, "[The] gold rush was, for the Indians, an overwhelming invasion of white, fortune-seeking scoundrels. These invaders, far from wanting to save Indian souls, were intent on uprooting all Indian obstacles for quick wealth. Within a few years, the California Indians were a besieged minority in a land that was once their own."[39]

At first, Native Americans joined in the search for gold. Some, such as the one thousand Yokuts who worked for a rancher near present-day Placerville, helped whites search for the precious metal. Others staked their own claims, and by the end of 1848 over four thousand Native Americans were working as gold miners. In addition, the fine baskets made by Na-

*Displaced from their traditional homelands, a group of Native Americans builds a small village called a rancheria on unclaimed ground.*

tive American women were suddenly in high demand by miners who used them to sift and pan for gold in rivers.

But the gold rush had extremely negative effects on the large majority of Native Americans. As tens of thousands of people flooded into the area from all over the world, the Native Americans acquired a new name, "Diggers," because of their practice of prying nutritious roots and bulbs from the soil with pointed sticks. But worse than ignorant racial epithets was the increase in lethal epidemics. In three short years, between 1849 and 1852, 15 percent, or fifteen thousand of California's one hundred thousand tribespeople, died from disease. And as more white miners flooded into the overcrowded gold fields, they did not hesitate to sell property, build towns, and establish farms on lands belonging to Native Americans.

Gold mining was also extremely destructive to the environment on which the tribes depended. Whereas most of California had been in a pristine natural state before 1849, the miners arrived with shovels, axes, and guns. They cut down tens of thousands of acres of forests for lumber. To mine gold they dug up streams and diverted the water, sometimes destroying hundreds of acres a week with high-powered hydraulic hoses. Once gold was found, it was treated with extremely toxic chemicals such as mercury and cyanide, and these dangerous wastes were later dumped in rivers.

Under this assault, salmon and other fish populations were severely impacted, while animals such as grizzly bears, wildcats, and other predators were driven by miners from the forests and hunted to near extinction. In addition, cattle, sheep, and other livestock trampled previously unspoiled fields that the tribes had tended for millennia.

As the gold rush continued, however, few Native Americans had time to worry about animals facing extinction. They themselves were dealing with an increasingly hostile population, some of whom were hunting tribespeople as if they were wild animals. As Indian agent Adam Johnson wrote:

> The majority of tribes are kept in constant fear on account of the indiscriminate and inhumane massacre of their people for real or supposed injuries. . . . I have seldom heard of a single difficulty between the whites and the Indians in which the original cause could not readily be traced to some rash or reckless act of the [white man]. In some instances it has happened that innocent Indians have been shot down for imaginary offenses which did not in fact exist. . . . When cattle were missing it was quickly supposed that they had been stolen by the Indians and the lives of several were paid. Again where a man was absent for a few days longer than expected his death was imagined and the lives of several [Indians] paid the penalty for the supposed murder.[40]

*California's first governor, Peter Burnett, signed a law that promoted the extinction of the Indian race.*

## An Infamous Law

In 1850 the California legislature passed a group of twenty laws known as "An Act for the Government and Protection of Indians." This legislation, far from offering protection, had the practical effect of legalizing the kidnapping and the enslavement of Native Americans in the state.

The first provision of the act stated that no "white man be convicted of any offense upon the testimony of an Indian or Indians."[41] This meant that anyone who robbed, assaulted, or murdered a Native American could not be jailed except in the unlikely event that some other white man (or woman) testified against the criminal. Other parts of the law addressed the Indians' labor position and had even more devastating effects, as Robert F. Heizer explains:

> [The 1850 law also] declared that any Indian, on the word of a White man, could be declared a vagrant, thrown in jail, and have his labor sold at auction for up to four months with no pay. This indenture law further said any Indian adult or child with the consent of his parents could be legally bound over to a White citizen for a period of years, laboring for subsistence only. These laws marked the transition of the Indian from peonage to virtual slavery. . . . Nearby Indians were rounded up, made to labor, and turned out to starve and die when the work season was over.[42]

This law essentially legalized the kidnapping of Native American children, a practice that became extremely common. Native tribes, enraged by these practices, retaliated by fighting off the white invaders with raids on their livestock and occasional violent attacks.

In 1851, after a few skirmishes in which whites were killed, the state of California set aside $1.1 million "for the suppression of Indian hostilities."[43] Upon signing the law, California's first governor, Peter H. Burnett stated: "That a war of extermination will continue to be waged between the two races until the Indian race becomes extinct, must be expected; while we cannot anticipate this result with but painful regret, the inevitable destiny of the race is beyond the power and wisdom of man to avert."[44]

These attitudes and laws, for all intents and purposes, encouraged white people to hunt Native Americans for sport. City governments distributed bounties, with some offering twenty-five cents to five dollars for Indian heads or scalps. In a state where thousands of miners were unemployed, such policies had disastrous consequences, and by 1870 there were only twenty thousand Native Americans surviving in California—a reduction of 80 percent since the gold rush began.

## Chapter 6

# Living in the United States of America

Ten thousand years of Native American culture in California was virtually destroyed in less than a century. Moreover, the twenty thousand or so people who had survived were at risk of being killed by vigilantes during the early years of California statehood.

In the 1850s the federal government in Washington, D.C., dispatched Indian commissioners to California to stop the wholesale slaughter and gain control over the situation. Backed by hundreds of U.S. Army soldiers, the commissioners called together tribal chiefs to negotiate treaties and formally take legal control of Native American lands. The negotiations were one-sided, however, as the Americans threatened to kill all men, women, and children if the leaders did not sign the treaties.

By 1852, 139 tribes had signed eighteen treaties granting the United States control of 92.5 percent of all California lands, leaving the tribes with 7.5 percent. In return the tribes were promised food, clothing, livestock, tools, and teachers who would instruct them in farming, carpentry, and so on. Despite these assurances, according to Robert F. Heizer, "These treaties enraged Whites, who bombarded Congress with an abusive campaign that resulted in their rejection."[45] The Senate then ordered the signed but inoperative treaties to be placed in secret files so that advocates for the Native Americans would have no access to them. The documents remained hidden from the public for fifty-three years.

Even without treaties, the federal government went ahead and created Indian reservations, or "farms." Congress appropriated about $350,000 for the task—about one-third the funds offered by the state to exterminate the tribespeople. Between 1856 and 1860 seven "Indian farms" were established in Central and Southern California in such places as the south end of the San Joaquin Valley, Tejon Pass, the Tule River, the foothills of the Sierras, and Fresno. Tribespeople were forced onto the land by brutal military men and vigilantes. Those who refused were shot.

Survivors who ended up on farms, besides fending off raids from bounty hunters who wanted to sell their scalps, were obliged to try to make a living without essential tools, medical care, and food, promised but not delivered by the government. Meanwhile, Indian agents, who oversaw the farms, worked the natives like slaves and sold the fruits of their labors on the open market, depriving the tribes of the necessities of life.

## Yokuts Tribesman Remembers Land Grab

In 1929 Frank F. Latta interviewed a 105-year-old Yokuts tribesman named Pahmit who recalled the arrival of the white Americans to his native lands during the gold rush when he was a young man in 1851. Pahmit's story was printed in *Handbook of Yokuts Indians:*

" 'First white man I see come mine gold in river. . . . Then lots white man come mine gold. After 'wile soldiers come, make big wood house [a fort] for fight. They all got gun. They catch lots Indian. Some Indian get 'way. Mokes (women), children run 'way, sleep in mountain under rock, brush. . . .

After big wood house done, soldier come with big man from Washington, sign paper with Indians. . . . Major [James D.] Savage come. . . . He have blue clothes. He have six, seven men. They all have blue clothes. They all got gun; they all soldier. Major Savage he talk my grandpa, Tomkit. He tell him big father at Washington send him see Indians. He say we haf bring all Indian chief here talk big man from Washington. . . . My grandpa, Tomkit, talk rest our chief. They think that's bad business. . . .

Then Major Savage . . . say, "I big medicine man with big father at Washington. You haf do what I say. I hurt you if I want to. I make all your people die. I make all fish go out river. I make all antelope, all elk go 'way. I make dark. You do what I say, nothing hurt you. . . .

He say we got give big Father at Washington all our land. We got go down valley, live. He say big white Father at Washington send us clothes; send us flour, send us blanket, send us horse. He say big white Father send us teacher, so our people go school like white man.

Our people no like that. They think all right send things. They no like go down valley. No acorns there; too many Indian there. . . . Then white man come; they mine gold in river. They shoot Indian. Soldier put Indian in jail; they whip Indian.' "

*A group of Native Americans stands outside their adobe home on an Indian farm in Central California.*

Although slavery was formally outlawed in the United States by the passage of the Thirteenth Amendment to the Constitution in 1865, little changed for the Native Americans. In 1870, however, the government itself gave up reservation oversight and turned operations over to the Society of Friends, the Quakers, and later the Methodists and Baptists. During the so-called Quaker Era there was less corruption on reservations, but the churches were extremely intolerant of traditional native beliefs. Once again, tribes were forced to renounce whatever remained of their cultural roots, languages, and religious beliefs in order to be "Christianized" and "Americanized."

## A Place to Call Home

By the 1880s some white Californians were finally becoming aware of the harm that had been done to the native tribes, partly because of a study entitled "The Report on the Condition and Needs of the Mission Indians of California," by Helen Hunt Jackson and Abbot Kinney, special agents to the Commission of Indian Affairs. In the report, the authors observed the lives of the twenty-nine hundred surviving Serrano, Cahuilla, Luiseño, and Diegueño who lived in California's three southernmost counties. The authors wrote that:

> Indian villages in the mountain valleys . . . freer from the contaminating influence of the white race, are industrious, peaceable communities, cultivating ground, keeping stock, carrying on their own simple manufactures of pottery, mats, baskets, &c., and making their living,—a very poor living, it is true; but they are independent and self-respecting in it, and ask nothing at the hands of the United States Government now, except that it will protect them in the ownership of their lands.[46]

Despite the sobering information in the Jackson-Kinney report, however, the

## A Legal Land Grab

A 1883 study by Helen Hunt Jackson and Abbot Kinney, "The Report on the Condition and Needs of the Mission Indians of California," found on the *linkLINE Communications* website, describes a typical situation in which white settlers simply buy out the land from under the tribes with the help of the Indian agent ostensibly there to protect Native American interests:

"In 1878 one of these special agents, giving an account of the San Pasquale Indians, mentioned the fact that a white man had just pre-empted the land on which the greater part of the village was situated. He had paid the price of the land to the register of the district land office. . . . 'He [admitted],' the agent says, 'that it was hard to wrest from these well-disposed and industrious creatures the homes they had built up; but,' said he, 'if I had not done it, somebody else would; for all agree that the Indian has no right to public lands.' This San Pasquale village was a regularly organized Indian pueblo, formed by about one hundred neophytes of the San Luis Rey Mission. . . . The record of its founding is preserved in the Mexican archives at San Francisco. These Indians had herds of cattle, horses, and sheep; they raised grains, and had orchards and vineyards. The whole valley in which this village lay was at one time set off by Executive order as a reservation, but by the efforts of designing men the order was speedily revoked; and no sooner has this been done than the process of dispossessing the Indians began. There is now, on the site of that old Indian pueblo, a white settlement numbering 35 voters. The Indians are all gone—some to other villages; some living near-by in cañons and nooks in the hills, from which, on the occasional visits of the priest, they gather and hold services in the half-ruined adobe chapel built by them in the days of their prosperity."

government continued to institute programs to turn "wild Indians" into average American farmers. In 1887 Congress passed the Dawes General Allotment Act, the terms of which granted each Native American family on a reservation an individual parcel of 160 acres of land. It was believed that if each man farmed his own private plot of land, he could make a profit, support his family, and join white society. This was in contradiction to the traditional communal ownership of lands, however, and written into the law were provisions that if the family did not make use of the land for agricultural purposes, then it would be taken from them. This posed a problem for the Southern California tribes because most of the land they occupied was too barren to be of any use for those practicing American farming methods. The government went ahead with its plan, and although the tribes resisted, individual allotments were given out at the Southern California Rincon, Morongo, and Pala reservations in 1893.

Ironically, just as the government was trying to encourage land ownership among tribespeople, they were denying the Cupeño, who resided at Warner Springs in San Diego County, the right to purchase the land they had lived on for centuries. Unfortunately non-Indians also desired the Warner Springs land, rich in natural resources and the site of the popular Agua Caliente hot springs. When officials attempted to evict the Cupeño, the courts sided with the tribe. The case was then appealed to the U.S. Supreme Court, however, and in 1902 the Cupeño were ordered from their ancestral home. When told of this decision, Cupeño leader Cecilio Blacktooth stated: "You see that graveyard out there? There are our fathers and grandfathers. . . . You see that Eagle-nest mountain and that Rabbit-hole mountain? When God made them, He gave us this place. . . . There is no other place for us. . . . If you will not buy this place we will go into the mountains like quail, and die there. . . . We do not want any other home."[47]

## Seeking Justice

Although the American legal system had opposed the Cupeño claims, as the twentieth century progressed, the tribes continued to fight for their rights in the courts. In 1905 the treaties that had been held in secret since 1852 were discovered by clerks working in the Senate archives. This finding inspired the tribes to begin agitating for land, goods, and services that had been promised in the treaties. This process would take years, however, and it was not until 1924 that a special commission was formed by the Bureau of Indian Affairs to study the matter. In 1944, more than ninety years after the treaties were signed, a federal court ruled that the tribes were entitled to $17.5 million for the 7 million acres that were illegally withheld from their possession. Tribespeople, however, only received a fraction of the monies. The government deducted $12 million for what it had given the tribes over the years, leaving only $5.5 million, or $150 apiece, for

## The Last Yahi

By the early years of the twentieth century, most Californians believed that the last of the "wild Indians" had long ago disappeared. But as the following article in *U.S. News & World Report* by Andrew Curry explains, there was one last member of the Yahi tribe practicing the old ways:

"The mysterious figure stumbled out of California's Cascade mountains in 1911, exhausted and clad only in a worn piece of canvas. Handcuffed by the Butte County sheriff, the 'wild man' was soon taken to the University of California's anthropology museum in San Francisco. Researchers pieced together his story and named him Ishi, 'man' in his language. He was a member of the Yahi, an American Indian tribe that had been ravaged by white bounty hunters . . . during the California gold rush era. His father was killed in a massacre in 1865, but Ishi and a handful of others survived in hiding for more than 40 years.

Dubbed 'the last wild Indian of America,' Ishi was the object of much fascination for eager researchers, who studied him as an anthropological specimen, putting him on display for hundreds of curious tourists. . . .

Ishi thrilled the tourists. He built a traditional hut on the museum grounds, chipped arrowheads, and started fires with sticks. He also adapted to life in early-20th-century San Francisco—he grew accustomed to wearing suits and ties and was fascinated by streetcars."

the roughly thirty-six thousand tribespeople now living in the state.

Meanwhile, every study of tribal life concluded that the natives of California were among the poorest people anywhere in the United States. In the first years of the century an embarrassed Bureau of Indian Affairs set aside hundreds of thousands of dollars to provide California's Native Americans with badly needed health care, and in 1901 the first "Indian Hospital" in the state was established in Riverside, east of Los Angeles. Funds were also used to enlarge reservations and improve water systems, especially in the driest southern counties where access to water was the difference between life and death.

## Termination and Relocation

Despite this small victory, the federal government continued to establish policies meant to weaken the tribes. In 1948 a policy called termination was instituted so that the government could terminate all services to Native Americans and turn

*President Calvin Coolidge stands on the South Lawn of the White House with the Commissioner of Indian Affairs, Charles Burke, and members of the Montana Blackfoot tribe.*

responsibility for the reservations over to the states. This allowed the government to revoke tribal status and, at the same time, begin taxing their lands. California tribes were the first to be terminated, but, according to Dwight Dutschke in "A History of American Indians in California" on the *Office of Historic Preservation* website, a state senate study showed "that most reservations were simply unprepared for termination, with a multitude of problems often including undefined boundaries, no roads, no water, no sanitation, substandard housing, and 2,600 complicated [ownership] cases."[48]

With such powerful state politicians against the plan, termination was never fully instituted on California reservations. The plan was put in place in other states, however, and in the late 1950s and early 1960s, from sixty to seventy thousand Native Americans from all over the United States—more than half of all relocated Indians in the country—migrated to Los Angeles, San Francisco, and other California cities. These newcomers greatly outnumbered California's struggling indigenous people, and the Native American population of the state was now swelled by Ojibwa and Oglala from Minnesota, Cherokee and

Choctaw from Oklahoma, and thousands of representatives from dozens of other tribes across the nation.

There was one bright spot during this time of termination and relocation: In 1963 the tribes won another lawsuit and received $46 million in payment for 65 million acres taken from them over the years. While this was a considerable sum of money, it totaled only forty-five cents an acre for land that by this time was worth billions, if not trillions, of dollars.

## A New Era

By the late 1960s America was changing rapidly. The successes of the African American civil rights movement inspired women, Hispanics, and other interest groups to seek equality and an end to discrimination. Native Americans also took part in this revolution; theirs is known as the Red Power Movement.

In 1969 the Native American Studies Department was established at the University of California at Berkeley, Davis, and Los Angeles. For the first time, Native American cultures were explored in a respectful, scholarly way at institutions of higher learning. Robert F. Heizer writes, "As a result, considerable academic research has been done in areas generally totally neglected by the academic community. . . . The programs offer good opportunities for Indian students to train themselves in various professions that could be important to the future of Indian tribes and communities."[49]

Despite such gains, throughout the 1970s California tribes continued to face the same problems they had for centuries. A state report issued in the early seventies stated that on reservations, 50 percent of Indian housing was inadequate, 70 percent lacked proper sewage disposal, and 42 percent of the households were forced to use water from contaminated sources. These problems were aggravated by the fact that the average person on the reservation had an annual income of only twenty three hundred dollars, less than half of that earned by non-Indians at that time.

## Indian Gaming

The grim statistics concerning the tribes changed almost overnight in 1988 with the passage of the Indian Gaming Regulatory Act (IGRA), which legalized so-called Indian gaming, or casino-style gambling on reservations. Within a few years, large glitzy casinos opened at dozens of Indian reservations and rancherias in California.

Indian gambling, originally a part of tribal ceremonies or celebrations, existed long before Europeans came to America. Men and women made dicelike gambling instruments from walnut shells, sticks, and seashells. Native Americans bet on foot races, archery, javelin throwing, and other endurance contests as well as horse races. Often Olympic-style games were played between villages and other tribes. Bettors wagered clothing, weapons, blankets, ornaments, and medals.

With the legalization of Indian gaming in the late 1980s, the native tribes of California received a golden opportunity that had come their way, the first since the Spanish

## Going Back to Alcatraz

In November 1969 eighty-nine Native Americans drew attention to the plight of American Indians when they took over Alcatraz Island in San Francisco Bay. Citing a clause in a long-forgotten one hundred-year-old treaty that said any abandoned forts, prisons, or other federal lands must revert to Indian use, the tribes moved onto the twelve-acre island, which was the location of the infamous Alcatraz Federal Prison until 1963. This takeover drew worldwide media attention.

In a move steeped in humor and satire, the occupying tribes sent a letter to the government—and the press—offering to set up a Bureau of Caucasian Affairs to guide white people in the proper manner of living, and offering to teach them Indian religion, education, and lifestyles to save whites from a savage and unhappy life.

Over the course of the next nineteen months, over fifty-six hundred Native Americans from nearly every state in the nation sailed the short distance from the San Francisco wharf to Alcatraz. Some stayed a day, some stayed for months. They brought food, ceremonial items, and prayer. Politicians, wealthy entertainers, reporters, Black Panthers, Girl Scout troops, and members of women's groups braved Coast Guard blockades to protest on Alcatraz with the Native Americans.

By June 1971, with the government threatening imminent action, only fourteen people remained on the island. On June 11 federal marshals reclaimed Alcatraz and removed the last of the occupants.

Although the occupation was over, a new era of Native American activism was born, and Indian leaders cited at least ten major shifts in federal law after the protest, including the Indian Self Determination and Education Act to better educate Native Americans and the passage of the Indian Health Act.

had arrived in 1769. By 2000, 80 of the state's 112 tribes had opened casinos that generated $5 billion in revenue annually. And the money earned from these casinos allowed tribal governments, for the first time, to overturn more than two centuries of poverty and federal neglect on reservations.

Although some believe Indian gaming has made the average Native American rich, tribes are utilizing most of the profits to pay off costs incurred to go into gaming, such as building casinos, hotels, restaurants, and roads. The rest of the money is going toward building self-sufficiency and government infrastructure on reservations. Since IGRA allows only the tribal governments to enter into gaming (not individuals), the tribes are using their gaming profits for law enforcement, education, economic development, tribal courts, and infrastructure improvement such as building new houses, new schools, new roads, and new sewer and water systems. This money also benefits individuals by funding social service programs, scholarships, health care clinics, chemical dependency treatment programs, and other uses.

## Coming Around

The tribes also have not forgotten those who helped them when they were living in poverty. In San Diego, the Viejas band of Kumeyaay gives millions of dollars to organizations that care for the poor. The San Diego Food Bank, which helped the tribes when they were struggling with 80 percent unemployment less than twenty years ago, has been the beneficiary of tribal funds, organized collection drives, and Native American volunteer efforts.

As a brief article by an unnamed Kumeyaay author in the *San Diego Business Journal* states, "The San Diego Food Bank reached out to us and ensured that our families would not go hungry. We've never forgotten their generosity. . . . The members of the Viejas Band have known hunger and prosperity. Our compassion is integral to our identity. Caring for our community is not a choice. It is simply the way we have always lived."[50]

*Profits from Indian gaming casinos are reinvested into the infrastructure of the tribe, providing education, electricity, water, and health services.*

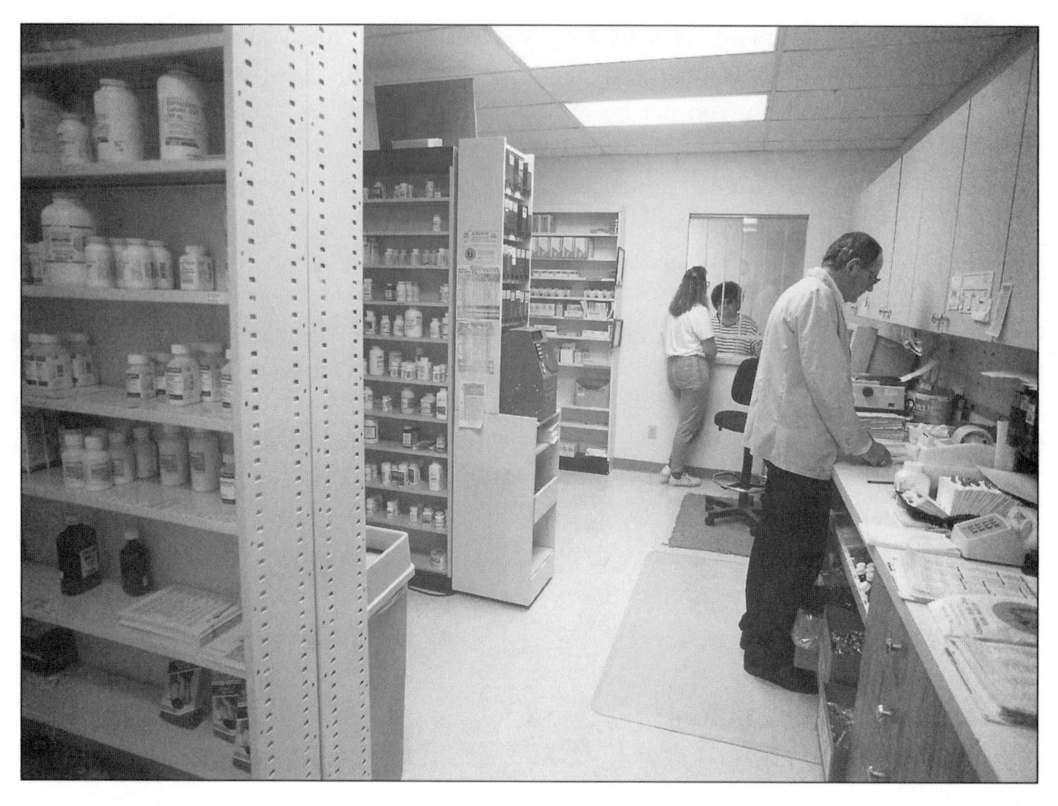

*The Viejas band of Kumeyaay used some of their gaming income to build a full-scale pharmacy as part of the health services for their tribe.*

In addition to this philanthropy, the Viejas tribe contributes millions to "nongaming" tribes that live in rural areas where it is impossible to operate successful casinos. The gaming tribes of California have also become huge political donors, gaining power and prestige among politicians by giving as much as $42 million since 1999 to senate and gubernatorial candidates.

## Bucking a Powerful Trend

While the casinos have benefited the tribes, there is powerful opposition to casino expansion. In 2000, for example, the Buena Vista Miwok—a tribe of six adults and six children—decided to build a sprawling $100 million casino on sixty-seven acres of rancheria land in Ione, California, south of Sacramento in the heart of what was once gold rush country. The tiny tribe, backed by wealthy East Coast investors, envisioned a casino with two thousand slot machines, several restaurants, a hotel, and a concert hall. But local farmers, ranchers, and environmentalists were fearful that a huge gambling center would destroy the rural character of their region. Some local tribes also opposed the operation; the Ione band of Miwok had long been burying its members at a sacred burial site where the proposed casino would be built.

## A Mix of Old and New

While the growth of the Indian gaming business has made headlines in recent years, a quieter revolution is taking place on reservations throughout the state. Once harassed and punished for practicing their cultural beliefs, modern tribespeople in California have revived many festivals and ceremonies from past centuries with vigor.

One such example is the Solstice Gathering, held in June on the Barona Reservation in San Diego County. On the longest day of the year, dancing and singing provide a backdrop to the celebration of ancient Kumeyaay culture. And the indigenous Californians hosting the festivities are joined by Native Americans from all over the country who now call the state their home. As Arizona native Debra Utacia Krol writes on her band's website, *pechanga.net*, the "Kumeyaay people treated us as long-lost kin. We spoke of our homes and customs while the women teased me. I'd lived in the Arizona desert so long, they said, that my head must be baked. . . . The music, the

*Native American dancers perform during a tribal festival on the Morongo Indian Reservation. Many Californian tribes are reviving such traditional festivals.*

acorn pudding, the gentle laughter of my cousins brought tears to my eyes. I was home."[51]

The Kumeyaay Bird Singers provide the music, singing several of the three hundred ancient songs that are said to have been among the first music composed in California. The songs use animal metaphors to transmit messages about history, customs, and moral values as well as food, the environment, and geography. They are accompanied by the shaking of gourds or tortoiseshell rattles filled with native palm seeds.

Many such gatherings are taking place throughout the state. In western Marin County, the Coastal Miwok have revived the annual spring Strawberry Festival at Kule Loklo, an uninhabited Miwok village reconstructed at Point Reyes National Seashore. Sponsored by the Federated Indians of Graton Rancheria in nearby Santa Rosa, the event lasts long into the night as Miwok, Wappo, and others dance, sing, and feast to celebrate the blessing of the strawberries. In *California Indian Country: The Land and the People*, Dolan H. Eargle Jr. describes the scene:

> Tables under the spreading laurel tree are laden with baskets of strawberries. The dancers step barefoot . . . to surround a roaring fire fanned by the wind. The eight women are wearing long dresses with embroidery, carrying Y-shaped garlands or wearing circular ones—all woven with fresh spring flowers. They also wear colorful beaded headbands festooned with dangling ornaments, symbolic of the California quail. A man wears an unusual headdress with two very tall, blue-feather "antlers." His movements are those of a very alert deer.
>
> The eldest of the elder ladies . . . bearing laurel branches and accompanied by singers, clapper sticks, and a drum, sings songs blessing the strawberries. Afterwards, she indicates that *everyone* is to partake of the extraordinarily generous offering of berries—the universal generosity of the Indian peoples.[52]

Perhaps the most popular Native American celebrations are powwows, a word derived from spiritual leaders who communicated with the spirits. In modern times, powwows are events where Native Americans gather to dance, sing, pray, play, socialize, and feast. Throughout the summer and fall, powwows are held in dozens of California locations from Eureka and Placerville in the north to San Diego in the south. One of the largest is the West Coast Powwow, a two-day event in Los Angeles that attracts more than ten thousand people from sixty tribes.

## Continuing Education

Such festivities serve to educate the general public to Native American cultural practices. And like many other tribes, the Miwok have embarked on a mission to teach the ancient ways to community members from many cultural backgrounds.

This is seen at Kule Loklo where the tribe's "California Indian Skills" classes teach Native American skills and crafts using traditional methods.

One class teaches students to tan deer hides into soft, washable buckskin while another instructs participants in the art of Pomo tule-reed basket weaving. Jewelers can learn to make Coast Miwok–style jewelry from clamshells and abalone, using traditional pump drills and sandstone grinding techniques. Others are instructed to make arrow, spear, and knife blades of obsidian using methods that have been used in California for thousands of years. In addition, classes are offered in the making of dyes, flutes and whistles, nets and cords, and acorn cookery.

While such classes help keep tradition alive, some Native American educators feel their most important task is to revitalize native languages. In 2002 the Pechanga band of the Luiseño Mission Indians joined with the University of California at Riverside to begin a program to teach the ancestral Luiseño language to a new generation of young tribemembers. The effort has taken on new urgency because about half of California's approximately one hundred tribal languages are nearly extinct. This is

*A Hupa woman teaches a child the art of weaving baskets from straw. Passing along such knowledge ensures the continued practice of traditional customs and crafts.*

troublesome to Gary DuBois, director of Pechanga Cultural Resources, who states:

> With the death of ancestral languages, the process of comprehending one's own history and describing the landscape is changed. . . . The intimate descriptions of nature and human relations, which were once locked in the native language, no longer exist and must be translated through the dominant language. Therefore, it becomes impossible to transmit fundamental cultural ways of knowing across the generations.
>
> Guided by our elders, Pechanga decided to try to do something about this situation. . . . Learning Luiseño is an important part of being Luiseño.[53]

Tribe members hope to use the program as a model to revitalize other languages such as the Serrano language spoken by only one remaining native speaker at the Morongo Reservation of Riverside County.

## Into a New Century

In the twenty-first century, a large percentage of California's 1 million Native Americans speak English. And as reservations have been given over to casinos, the ma-

*A Native American storyteller teaches children the culture and history of their tribe through traditional stories and songs.*

jority of these people live in urban areas. For example there are at least one hundred thousand Native Americans in Los Angeles alone—a number that grew 30 percent between 1980 and 1990. While most of these people can trace their roots to tribes outside of California, they make up one of the fastest-growing minority populations in the state.

The Native Americans of California lived in a paradise of peace and prosperity for thousands of years. Within months of the Spanish incursion, tribespeople began to die in large numbers as a result of disease. The institutionalized slavery, greed, prejudice, and hatred of the Spanish missions and the American gold rush steered these once bountiful people near total extinction.

Although eight out of ten tribespeople were wiped out within two generations, survivors struggled to maintain their rich cultural heritage in the face of widespread murderous hostility. Only in recent years has the power of American capitalism come to their aid, setting off another kind of gold rush at casinos throughout the region. With this new wealth, the voices of Native Americans can once again be heard echoing through the rural canyons—and the capitol buildings in Sacramento and Washington, D.C. After a long, brutal, bloody journey through the settlement of America's richest state, the native tribes of California may have finally entered a new age at the dawn of the twenty-first century. As Debra Utacia Krol eloquently states:

> Although many of us don't have land, and those who do possess only a tiny piece of their ancestral homes, we have labored mightily to preserve what is left: our languages, our cultures, our precious sense of identity and belonging. . . .
>
> [And] casinos are only a fraction of what California Indians are about. We are the caretakers of a heritage stretching back over 10,000 years, a people both proud and impoverished by the abuses of a brutal occupancy.
>
> Yet hope springs from the black earth, the giant oaks, the green hills of Barona. You can see it in the bustling businesses that finance the Kumeyaay's efforts to repatriate ancestors and artifacts. And in the proud faces and stances of tribal members old and young. It's clear these people intend Kumeyaay country to prevail another 10,000 years.[54]

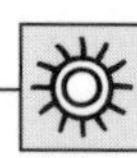

# Notes


**Introduction: The First Californians**

1. Quoted in Robert F. Heizer and Alan F. Almquist, *The Other Californians*. Berkeley: University of California Press, 1971, p. 2.

**Chapter 1: Tribes of California**

2. Maureen Bell, *Karuk: The Upriver People*. Happy Camp, CA: Naturegraph, 1991, p. 7.
3. A.L. Kroeber, *Handbook of the Indians of California*. New York: Dover, 1976, p. 160.
4. Marie Potts, *The Northern Maidu*. Happy Camp, CA: Naturegraph, 1977, pp. 7–8.
5. Malcolm Margolin, *The Ohlone Way*. Berkeley, CA: Heyday Books, 1978, p. 1.
6. Kroeber, *Handbook of the Indians of California*, p. 474.
7. Kroeber, *Handbook of the Indians of California*, p. 551.
8. Kroeber, *Handbook of the Indians of California*, p. 621.
9. From an article in Robert F. Heizer, ed., *California*, vol. 8 of *Handbook of North American Indians*. Washington, D.C.: Smithsonian Institution, 1978, p. 551.

**Chapter 2: Village Life in Southern California**

10. Kroeber, *Handbook of the Indians of California*, p. 79.
11. Margolin, *The Ohlone Way*, p. 15.
12. Margolin, *The Ohlone Way*, p. 13.
13. Quoted in Frank F. Latta, *Handbook of Yokuts Indians*. Santa Cruz, CA: Bear State Books, 1977, p. 368.
14. From an article in Heizer, *California*, p. 447.
15. Harry C. James, *The Cahuilla Indians*. Los Angeles: Westernlore Press, 1960, p. 48.
16. Quoted in Lowell John Bean, *Mukat's People: The Cahuilla Indians of Southern California*. Berkeley: University of California Press, 1972, p. 33.
17. Michael Baksh, "The Kumeyaay," *Daphne*. http://daphne.palomar.edu.
18. Margolin, *The Ohlone Way*, p. 103.
19. Margolin, *The Ohlone Way*, p. 104.

**Chapter 3: A Land of Plenty**

20. Margolin, *The Ohlone Way*, p. 43.
21. Baksh, "The Kumeyaay."
22. Miguel Costansó, *The Discovery of San Francisco Bay*, ed. Peter Browning. Lafayette, CA: Great West Books, 1992, p. 33.
23. Robert F. Heizer and Albert B. Elsasser, *The Natural World of the California Indians*. Berkeley: University of California Press, 1980, pp. 106–107.
24. Margolin, *The Ohlone Way*, pp. 100–101.

25. Quoted in Lowell J. Bean and Thomas C. Blackburn, *Native Californians.* Socorro, NM: Ballena Press, 1976, p. 297.

**Chapter 4: Spirits and Healing**

26. Malcolm Margolin, ed., *The Way We Lived.* Berkeley: Heyday Books, 1981, p. 140.
27. Fernando Librado, *Breath of the Sun.* Banning, CA: Malki Museum Press, 1979, p. 124.
28. Bernice Eastman Johnston, *California's Gabrielino Indians.* Los Angeles: Southwest Museum, 1962, pp. 60–61.
29. Johnston, *California's Gabrielino Indians*, pp. 63–64.
30. Margolin, *The Ohlone Way*, p. 76.
31. William Duncan Strong, *Aboriginal Society in Southern California.* Banning, CA: Malki Museum Press, 1987, p. 172.
32. *The Muwekma Ohlone.* www.muwekma.org.

**Chapter 5: Clash of Cultures**

33. From an article in Heizer, *California*, p. 547.
34. Daniel Fogel, *Junípero Serra, the Vatican, and Enslavement Theology.* San Francisco: Ism Press, 1988, p. 52.
35. Joel R. Hyer, *"We Are Not Savages."* East Lansing: Michigan State University Press, 2001, pp. 24–25.
36. Fogel, *Junípero Serra, the Vatican, and Enslavement Theology*, p. 151.
37. Quoted in Heizer, *California*, p. 105.
38. Fogel, *Junípero Serra, the Vatican, and Enslavement Theology*, p. 159.
39. Fogel, *Junípero Serra, the Vatican, and Enslavement Theology*, p. 159.
40. Quoted in Heizer, *California*, p. 107.
41. Quoted in Dwight Dutschke, "A History of American Indians in California: 1849–1879," Office of Historic Preservation, July 29, 1999. www.ohp.parks.ca.gov.
42. Heizer, *California*, p. 108.
43. Quoted in Dutschke, "A History of American Indians in California: 1849–1879."
44. Quoted in Thorne B. Gray, *The Stanislaus Indian Wars.* Modesto, CA: The McHenry Museum Press, 1993, p. xxv.

**Chapter 6: Living in the United States of America**

45. Heizer, *California*, p. 109.
46. Helen Hunt Jackson and Abbot Kinney, "The Report on the Condition and Needs of the Mission Indians of California," linkLINE Communications. http://linkline.com.
47. Quoted in Hyer, *"We Are Not Savages,"* p. 77.
48. Quoted in Dwight Dutschke, "A History of American Indians in California: 1934–1964," *Office of Historic Preservation*, July 29, 1999. www.ohp.parks.ca.gov.
49. Heizer, *California*, pp. 125–26.
50. *San Diego Business Journal*, "The Viejas Band Of Kumeyaay Indians," July 16, 2001, p. 23.
51. Debra Utacia Krol, "Field Trip Proves California's Indians Are Alive and

Dancing," July 18, 2002. http://pechanga.net.

52. Dolan H. Eargle Jr., *California Indian Country: The Land and the People*. San Francisco: Trees Company Press, 1992, p. 55.
53. Quoted in Black Voice News, "Native Languages to Be Revitalized Through UCR," New California Media, July 12, 2002. http://news.ncmonline.com.
54. Krol, "Field Trip Proves California's Indians Are Alive and Dancing."

# For Further Reading

Lowell John Bean and Lisa L. Bourgeault, *The Cahuilla.* New York: Chelsea House, 1989. The history and culture of the tribes who made their home in the southeastern California deserts.

Mary Null Boulé, *California Native American Tribes.* Books 3, 4, 5, 6, 9, 14, 18, 21, 23, 24, and 26. Vashon, WA: Merryant, 1992. Short books about individual tribes such as the Cahuilla, Chumash, Diegueño, Gabrielino, Ohlone, Yokut, and others that are part of a twenty-six-book series on California Indians.

George Emanuels, *California Indians: An Illustrated Guide.* Lemoore, CA: Kings River Press, 1992. The culture, history, and everyday life of sixteen major California tribes with over 150 illustrations and maps.

Stephanie Lewis, *The Indians of California.* Alexandria, VA: Time-Life Books, 1994. A large, colorful book detailing the social customs, religious practices, history, and modern lives of the California tribes.

Martin Schwabacher, *The Chumash Indians.* New York: Chelsea House, 1995. A study of the Native American tribes who inhabited the present-day Santa Barbara region.

Linda Yamane and Dugan Aguilar, *Weaving a California Tradition: A Native American Basketmaker.* Minneapolis: Lerner, 1996. A photo-essay of an eleven-year-old girl as she is instructed in the art of basket making by her mother and aunts.

# Works Consulted

## Books


Eugene N. Anderson Jr., *The Chumash Indians of Southern California*. Banning, CA: Malki Museum Press, 1968. One in a series of brochures published by the Malki Museum concerning the lifestyles of tribes native to the region.

Lowell John Bean, *Mukat's People: The Cahuilla Indians of Southern California*. Berkeley: University of California Press, 1972. A scholarly study of the native tribes who inhabited the desert regions of southeast California.

Lowell J. Bean and Thomas C. Blackburn, *Native Californians*. Socorro, NM: Ballena Press, 1976. A series of articles by researchers and anthropologists concerning various details of Native American life.

Maureen Bell, *Karuk: The Upriver People*. Happy Camp, CA: Naturegraph, 1991. A study of the northwestern Karuk and their everyday lives of hunting, fishing, and religious celebrations.

Miguel Costansó, *The Discovery of San Francisco Bay*. Ed. Peter Browning. Lafayette, CA: Great West Books, 1992. A 1769 account of the Gaspar de Portolá expedition describing the natural wonders of the bay area and the Native Americans who inhabited the region.

Dolan H. Eargle Jr., *California Indian Country: The Land and the People*. San Francisco: Trees Company Press, 1992. California Native Americans in modern times, their art, architecture, festivals, sacred places, and music with a guide to the more than one hundred reservations in the state.

———, *The Earth is Our Mother*. San Francisco: Trees Company Press, 1986. A history of California's native tribes and a guide to their historical homelands and present-day reservations.

Daniel Fogel, *Junípero Serra, the Vatican, and Enslavement Theology*. San Francisco: Ism Press, 1988. The detailed account of

California's first friar and how he used the mission system to mold the destiny of the state's native tribes through conversion and slavery.

Thorne B. Gray, *The Stanislaus Indian Wars*. Modesto, CA: The McHenry Museum Press, 1993. The story of the Laquisimas band of Northern Yokuts who mounted one of the most intense campaigns against the mission system of any California tribe.

Robert F. Heizer, ed., *California*. Vol. 8 of *Handbook of North American Indians*. Washington, D.C.: Smithsonian Institution, 1978. An in-depth exploration of California tribes with articles by nationally recognized experts in tribal history and culture.

Robert F. Heizer and Alan F. Almquist, *The Other Californians*. Berkeley: University of California Press, 1971. A book about the prejudice and discrimination Native Americans, Chinese, and Japanese faced from Spaniards and Americans in California.

Robert F. Heizer and Albert B. Elsasser, *The Natural World of the California Indians*. Berkeley: University of California Press, 1980. The native plants and animals of California and how they were utilized by the tribes to provide all necessary means of survival.

Joel R. Hyer, *"We Are Not Savages."* East Lansing: Michigan State University Press, 2001. The history of the Cupeño, Luiseño, and Kumeyaay and their experiences on the Pala Reservation between 1840 and 1920. The author, an advocate for Native Americans, is Faculty Fellow of History at California State University, San Marcos.

Harry C. James, *The Cahuilla Indians*. Los Angeles: Westernlore Press, 1960. The history of the Native American tribe who inhabited the Mojave and other desert regions of southeastern California.

Bernice Eastman Johnston, *California's Gabrielino Indians*. Los Angeles: Southwest Museum, 1962. An exploration of the tribe that once thrived in the Los Angeles basin, with information gathered from eyewitness accounts, archeologists, and historians.

A.L. Kroeber, *Handbook of the Indians of California*. New York: Dover, 1976. An in-depth study of California natives with chapters on each major tribe and subdivision, covering law and customs, land and civilization, ethnic geography, religion, and other categories. First published in 1923 after the author spent seventeen years living among the state's native populations.

Frank F. Latta, *Handbook of Yokuts Indians*. Santa Cruz, CA: Bear State Books, 1977. One of the most detailed studies of the tribes of the San Joaquin watershed, originally published in 1949, with dozens of drawings and interesting photos from the early twentieth century.

Fernando Librado, *Breath of the Sun*. Banning, CA: Malki Museum Press, 1979. The firsthand recollections of a Chumash tribesman, written in 1912, describing nineteenth-century Indian life.

Malcolm Margolin, *The Ohlone Way*. Berkeley, CA: Heyday Books, 1978. A poetic study that invokes the long-ago lifestyles of the tribes that inhabited the region between San Francisco Bay and Monterey Bay.

Malcolm Margolin, ed., *The Way We Lived*. Berkeley: Heyday Books, 1981. Stories, songs, myths, and legends of California tribes on subjects such as growing up and the conflict of love, dreams, power, and death.

Marie Potts, *The Northern Maidu*. Happy Camp, CA: Naturegraph, 1977. The history of the tribes that once inhabited Yosemite, written by a Maidu woman born in 1895.

James J. Rawls, *Indians of California*. Norman: University of Oklahoma Press, 1984. An exploration of the negative stereotypes applied to California tribes by Europeans and Americans since the time of the Spanish settlement.

Hugo Reid, *The Indians of Los Angeles County*. Los Angeles: Southwest Museum, 1968. A series of articles, written for a local paper in 1852, that make up one of the most detailed records concerning the lives of the dwindling Native American population of Los Angeles.

William Duncan Strong, *Aboriginal Society in Southern California*. Banning, CA: Malki Museum Press, 1987. A scholarly study of the Cahuilla, Serrano, Luiseño, and other tribes, originally published in 1929 by one of the leading anthropologists of the day.

Clifford E. Trafzer and Joel R. Hyer, eds., *"Exterminate Them!"* East Lansing: Michigan State University Press, 1999. Newspaper stories and letters to the editor written between 1848 and 1868 document the murderous prejudice commonly vented against California's Native Americans during the gold rush.

**Periodicals**

Andrew Curry, "The Last of the Yahi," *U.S. News & World Report*, August 21, 2000. A story about Ishi, the last of the Yahi who followed the old ways until 1911 when he stumbled out of the woods and into the glare of civilization.

*San Diego Business Journal*, "The Viejas Band Of Kumeyaay Indians," July 16, 2001. A brief article about the philanthropic work of a tribe that has reaped untold wealth with its San Diego County casino.

**Internet Resources**

*American Indian Source.Com*, "Hatam and Kumeyaay History." www.americanindiansource.com. A site detailing events from the past and the situation in the present for the natives of San Diego County.

*bakersfield.com*, Tomo-Kahni State Park, "Kawaiisu Culture." www.bakersfield.com. A site dedicated to Kawaiisu history, language, shelter, diet, clothing, recreation, stories and myths, rock art, and more.

Michael Baksh, "The Kumeyaay," *Daphne*. http://daphne.palomar.edu. A site dedicated to the housing, agriculture, social organization, and other details of the tribes of San Diego County.

*Black Voice News*, "Native Languages to Be Revitalized Through UCR," *New California Media,* July 12, 2002. http://news.ncmonline.com. An article about new courses designed to teach the ancient Luiseño language to a new generation.

*Bureau of Land Management*, "Rock Art of Native California: A Visitor's Guide." www.ca.blm.gov. A site maintained by the federal government that provides information about Native American art found on many isolated public sites in California.

Dwight Dutschke, "A History of American Indians in California: 1849–1879," *Office of Historic Preservation*, July 29, 1999.

www.ohp.parks.ca.gov. Part of a comprehensive series of articles published by the California Department of Parks and Recreation Office of Historic Preservation.

———,"A History of American Indians in California: 1934–1964," *Office of Historic Preservation*, July 29, 1999. www.ohp.parks.ca.gov. Another part of the above series, this one covering the middle years of the twentieth century.

Helen Hunt Jackson and Abbot Kinney, "The Report on the Condition and Needs of the Mission Indians of California," linkLINE Communications. http://linkline.com. A website featuring the original 1883 report on the condition of Southern California tribes made by agents of the Commission of Indian Affairs.

Debra Utacia Krol, "Field Trip Proves California's Indians Are Alive and Dancing," *pechanga.net.*, July 18, 2002. http://pechanga.net. An article about the Solstice Gathering at the Barona Reservation in San Diego County.

**Website**

**The Muwekma Ohlone** (www.muwekma.org). A site compiled by eight tribal members detailing the cultural and geographical landscape of an Ohlone tribelet prior to Spanish contact.

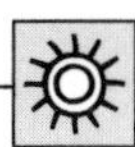

# Index

# Picture Credits

Cover Photo: © Catherine Karnow/CORBIS
© Tom Bean/CORBIS, 50
© Bettmann/CORBIS, 14, 55, 78
© Bowers Museum of Cultural Art/CORBIS, 23
© Ralph A. Clevenger/CORBIS
© CORBIS, 42, 72, 77, 82, 86
© Gianni Dagli Orti/CORBIS, 12
© Hal Horwitz/CORBIS
Stuart Kallen, 28, 35, 70
Library of Congress, 24, 27, 34, 36, 38, 41, 43, 45, 47, 52, 58, 59, 63, 75
Brandy Noon, 16
© Bob Rowan; Progressive Image/CORBIS, 89, 90, 91, 94
© Phil Schermeister/CORBIS, 29, 93
© Nik Wheeler/CORBIS, 68

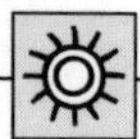

# About the Author

Stuart A. Kallen is the author of more than 150 nonfiction books for children and young adults. He has written on topics ranging from the theory of relativity to the history of rock and roll. In addition, Mr. Kallen has written award-winning children's videos and television scripts. In his spare time, Stuart A. Kallen is a singer/songwriter/guitarist in San Diego, California.